"Robin Barnett has a true gift for working with the toughest addicts and the families that love them. Her book *Addict in the House* is a blueprint for all families to follow when faced with addiction in the home."

> —**Heather R. Hayes, MEd, LPC, CIP**, intervention pioneer featured on *Dr. Oz*, international certified hostage negotiator, and cofounder of Hayes, Davidson and Associates

"Robin Barnett's experience with families struggling with an addict in the home is unparalleled, and her new book *Addict in the House* is an absolute must-read for anyone struggling with addiction, the people who love them, and most importantly, those who enable them!"

> —**Akikur Mohammad, MD**, is a board-certified psychiatrist in addiction medicine, an award-winning academic, professor in the department of psychiatry at the Keck School of Medicine of the University of Southern California, and author of *The Anatomy of Addiction*

"Robin Barnett's *Addict in the House* is a must-read for any family struggling to find answers and a workable strategy for dealing with addiction with someone they love."

> —**Josh Shipp**, television personality and author of *The Teen's Guide to World Domination*

"In a world wrought with more addiction nightmares than ever before, it is essential that families know how to respond and take action when confronted with addiction in the home. Robin Barnett's *Addict in the House* is a must-read for anyone looking for answers when addiction hits home."

> —**Loni Coombs**, television legal analyst, former prosecutor, and author of *You're Perfect and Other Lies Parents Tell* ·

"With a constant stream of addiction-related news, there is no shortage of people struggling for answers when faced with an addiction crisis. At last, there is a guide for families struggling to find answers, direction, and solutions. Robin Barnett's *Addict in the House* is a must-read for anyone and everyone caught in the struggle."

> —**Kimberly Cornell**, EMMY award-winning executive producer for KTLA and Tribune Broadcasting stations

"Robin Barnett is a true authority on the topics of addiction, addiction treatment, and family strategy. Her book *Addict in the House* is an absolute gift of knowledge and inspiration for all families struggling to find a solution *and* a workable plan when addiction rears its ugly head at home."

> —**Harry Phillips**, award-winning producer of ABC News, *20/20*, and *Nightline*

ADDICT

IN

the

HOUSE

A NO-NONSENSE FAMILY GUIDE THROUGH ADDICTION & RECOVERY

ROBIN BARNETT, EdD, LCSW

New Harbinger Publications, Inc.

Publisher's Note

This publication is designed to provide accurate and authoritative information in regard to the subject matter covered. It is sold with the understanding that the publisher is not engaged in rendering psychological, financial, legal, or other professional services. If expert assistance or counseling is needed, the services of a competent professional should be sought.

Distributed in Canada by Raincoast Books

Copyright © 2016 by Robin Barnett
New Harbinger Publications, Inc.
5674 Shattuck Avenue
Oakland, CA 94609
www.newharbinger.com

Cover design by Amy Shoup
Acquired by Melissa Kirk
Edited by Jennifer Eastman

Library of Congress Cataloging-in-Publication Data on file

Printed in the United States of America

18   17   16

10   9   8   7   6   5   4   3   2   1   First Printing

Contents

Foreword

I loathe the disease of addiction.

The National Institute on Drug Abuse recently estimated that the financial cost related to the abuse of tobacco, alcohol, and illicit drugs exceeds $700 billion dollars annually. This ridiculously enormous number reflects the financial drain related only to crime, lost work productivity, and health care—and in the United States alone.

While that number is indeed staggering, it seems so *sterile*, so *impersonal*, compared to the way I see addiction manifested on a daily basis. These numbers don't even begin to address the horrible ripple effect of addiction, the impact on other people driven by incarcerations, health crises, and premature deaths, the permanent scars that are suffered by generation after generation. And what these numbers can't begin to address is the loss of human potential, all the fantastic, spectacular things that will never be because of the scourge of addiction. The careers, the relationships, the contributions that will, quite simply, never happen.

What is most frustrating about it is that it doesn't have to be that way.

Of course, I know about all of this not just because I've studied it clinically and know about it intellectually. I know it because I've lived it.

As a kid, I always felt like I was on the outside looking in, like everyone else had an owner's manual to help them successfully navigate life's challenges, and I had been absent the day those were being handed out. It didn't help matters that I was a fat kid, desperately uncomfortable in my own skin.

Worse, because of my mom's recent remarriage(s), we had relocated from California to Oregon and then to Virginia, where we lived on the outskirts of a very affluent area. (When I say "outskirts," I mean a crappy apartment that just happened to be near the brick and white-column mansions my schoolmates lived in.) The kids who surrounded me went through life with a seeming grace and ease that I simply did not have. They wore boating shoes and shirts with little alligators and polo players on them, while I wore a brand of jeans from Sears called "Toughskins" in a size called "husky," also known as "loser fat-kid jeans." They did things that seemed totally alien to me, like showing up to class, studying Latin, and doing homework.

As a twelve-year-old, in seventh grade, I was assigned the project of writing a career report in one of my classes. The cover page of that report is framed and hangs in my office today. The overly neat cursive writing of a junior high school student reads: "This is a story of what I, Darren Kavinoky, will be like ten years from now. Or, rather, a speculation of what I will be like ten years from now. I feel that while a person's physical features may change, their basic psyche stays the same. If my philosophy holds true, I will probably be a bum. Or even worse, a lawyer. *Either way, you end up drinking something out of a brown paper bag. The only difference is where.*"

Oddly prophetic, since at that time I hadn't had a drink or anything else that was mind or mood altering (other than junk food!), but clearly I needed something.

All of that changed just one year later. I was then a thirteen-year-old, still wearing husky-size Toughskins, but I found myself at a party that I had no business being at, since all the "cool kids" were there. A few of the really cool guys were passing around a joint; one of them passed it my way. I wish I could tell you that I had a crisis of conscience in that moment. I wish I could tell you that the warnings of my parents, teachers, or any form of "Just say no!" crossed my mind. But that would be a lie. Because if you felt about yourself like I felt about myself, and one of the cool kids offered you a joint, there was nothing to do but take it.

In that one moment, everything changed. In that one moment, I no longer felt like I was on the outside looking in. Because of that moment, I could now hang with the cool guys and tell some jokes, and they'd laugh. Because of that moment, I could now talk to the pretty girls whom I had always wanted to talk to but couldn't. Because of that one moment, I no longer felt the button of my husky-size Toughskins jabbing me in the belly. I no longer felt the unbearable weight of just being me.

In that moment, I remember my thirteen-year-old brain consciously thinking, *I'm going to feel like this every moment from now on.* And for the next twenty years, almost to the day, I made good on that promise.

One of the lessons I'm now painfully aware of is that we can never accurately calculate the cost of our misbehavior, but it is always greater than we calculate it to be. It must be this way; if I could accurately see the future costs, I wouldn't misbehave. But the seeds of denial are sown and reaped at lightning speed. In my case, that meant ever-declining grades in high school, flunking out of college, and getting arrested five different times (in three different countries) for various misbehaviors, all related to my being loaded.

The 1990s turned out to be an unpleasant decade for me, as I began to appreciate that I was the common denominator in all of my problems and that what had once been the solution to my problem—drugs and alcohol—had now boomeranged on me and was itself the problem. By this time, I needed drugs and alcohol like a drowning man needs air, and I would do anything to avoid the unthinkable for an addict: running out. I was in and out of five different treatment centers and, after each one of them, fell victim to the self-destructive thinking that so typifies the mental state of the alcoholic or addict.

Until another pivotal moment.

At this point in my life, I was basically homeless, and my wife (who had thrown me out a couple of years before) was allowing me to stay in her house (what used to be *our* house) only out of the goodness of her heart.

I sat in her study one night, reading a book about recovery. Since I was reading, it only made sense that a joint was burning in the ashtray and some Crown Royal on the rocks sat within inches of my trembling hands. As my wife passed by and saw this, she spoke the words that would change my life: "Aren't you supposed to be sober when you read that book?"

In that one moment, I could see myself with a clarity that was new and powerful. In that one moment, I knew that if I didn't change, I was a dead man walking. That moment happened on May 9, 2000, and I'm blessed to say I've not had any mind- or mood-altering substances since.

The power of a human being to transform is truly awe-inspiring. In my case, the fat kid in husky-size Toughskins has now completed seven Ironman triathlons and fits easily into normal-size clothes. The bankrupt attorney who was homeless now has a successful law firm that employs dozens of people and helps thousands. The selfish husband whose wife threw him out (deservedly!) has now celebrated twenty years of marriage to that amazing woman. And the best part is that I now have a teenage daughter who has never seen her daddy under the influence of anything.

To say that I'm glad you found this book is a tremendous understatement. The entire trajectory of my life changed because of one night when I sat reading a book, and someone cared enough to tell me the truth. There is no doubt in my mind that change happens in a moment, and if you are holding this book, whether it is because you suffer from addiction or care for someone who does, the power to change is in your hands. Godspeed.

—Darren Kavinoky

Introduction

On a snowy winter night in 1994, I got the call. My brother was reaching out for help—again.

For years, I had watched my family being ripped apart by his addiction. It had taken me to places I never imagined going: seedy motels, jails, mental hospitals. Like the rest of my family, I was trying my best to save someone I loved very much, always unsure in my heart whether he'd ever recover. We stood by him through rehab after rehab and detox after detox. We suffered many sleepless nights and developed a gut-level fear of the sound of a ringing telephone. Was it him calling for help again—or someone who needed me to identify his body?

On this night, it was him. What he said was a variation on a familiar theme. "I'm going to die out here." His voice was desperate, demanding. "I'm sleeping on a park bench."

A familiar flood of fear, guilt, anger, and panic washed over me. But this time, the flood brought something new: a clear sense of the right thing to do. In that instant, I realized that I could no longer participate in his addiction. I told him, "I will always love you, but until you decide to live, I cannot help anymore."

With that, I hung up the phone—and immediately began to shake in panic, thinking that if he died, I would be responsible. Had I really just turned my back on my big brother—the only person who truly shared and understood my experience? When my rational side kicked in, I knew that I had made my choice not to abandon him but to save myself.

I also knew that the same choice—to save himself—was available to him. He had become very treatment savvy; he knew the system better than I did. If he wanted help, he knew exactly where to find it. I recognized that I didn't control his life or his death. I let him make his own choice.

Why I Wrote This Book

My realization that night set me free. It also started me on the path that ultimately led me to write this book—the one I wish I'd had back when my brother's troubles began. *Addict in the House* brings together the knowledge, education, and experiences I've gained in two and a half decades of dealing with addiction.

Those lessons were learned first as a sister, then as a psychotherapist, then as cofounder of a drug- and alcohol-treatment facility in New Jersey, and now as an addiction specialist on nationally syndicated television. For me, addiction treatment is more than a career. It's the core of my life and my family's life. My goal is to share my knowledge with you so you can learn to live again—and help your addicted loved one decide to do the same.

How This Book Will Help You

Caring about someone with an addiction—whether it's your spouse, teenage daughter, parent, uncle, cousin, or anyone else in your life—can be a frustrating, exhausting experience. Your attempts to help only seem to make things worse. And just when you start feeling hopeful, the rug gets pulled out from under you. When you're not scared for your loved one, you're angry about what he's done to himself and your family. (And a lot of the time, you're both.)

In such a confusing landscape, it can be hard to know where you stand, let alone where to turn next. This book is your guide, laying out a clear path toward a less fearful, more satisfying life.

This book covers drug and alcohol addictions. All the stories and examples are from real alcoholics and drug addicts. And all of the advice and strategies for coping with and moving beyond these addictions have successfully helped thousands of family members like you. If your loved one is facing a different addiction—such as gambling, tobacco, or sex—I urge you to find a reputable source for the specific addiction, as those have special concerns and treatment options that aren't discussed in these pages. That said, all of the strategies discussed here are designed to help the family member regain a joyful, satisfying life are beneficial to all, no matter the type of addiction your loved one is facing.

I begin this book by defining addiction and exploring how it starts, so you can begin to understand your loved one's behavior, the reasons for relapse, and the hurdles to recovery. Then I'll discuss the best ways to help your loved one—including how to recognize when it's smarter to pull back.

We'll explore all the major treatment options, as well as resources for ongoing support. I'll also discuss special consider-ations for young addicts, from emotional development to legal issues.

The fear and anger generated by an addiction radiates well beyond the addict's life; you might not realize how much it has influenced your own behavior and beliefs. The second half of the book focuses on rebuilding your relationships and forging a more independent life.

Every chapter ends with an exercise that lets you put your new knowledge to work right away. Throughout the book, I'll also be sharing more of my own story—how my family has coped with my brother's addiction and his long struggle to beat it.

When you've completed this book, you'll be able to

- help your loved one get sober without overburdening yourself;

- distinguish between effective and ineffective forms of support;

- communicate more effectively with your loved one and other family members about addiction;

- help your loved one choose the best treatment options and get ongoing support;

- set and maintain firm boundaries that protect your well-being;

- begin your own recovery from the effects of addiction (and connect with others who are doing the same); and

- live a more gratifying life, whether your loved one stays sober or not.

The Journey Starts Today

My brother's battle isn't over. As I write this, he has been clean for four and a half years. Every day, I wake up with hope for him and for the millions of people around the world who are struggling with addiction.

Just as importantly, I live a rich, satisfying life that doesn't depend on his condition. I didn't reach this point on my own. I made it here with the help of all the addicts and families I've worked with, as well as the professionals I've studied under and collaborated with, over the past twenty-five years. I don't want you to wait that long, so I've condensed what I know into the next ten chapters.

It won't be an easy journey, and I'm sure we'll learn more along the way. But together, I know we can move toward a healthier, happier life. Let's get started.

CHAPTER 1

Understanding Addiction

One night in high school, I watched Chris stagger to our front door. His friends had dropped him off. The next day he had a bad hangover, and our parents grounded him, but nothing else came of it. He drank and smoked pot in college, but that hardly seemed uncommon. Even after college, when his friends stopped partying, but he continued, it didn't seem like a big deal. He seemed like the same brother I'd always known.

In my therapy practice and personal life, I've spoken with thousands of people who, like me, care deeply about someone who is addicted to drugs or alcohol. If there's one experience we all share, it's exasperation. Watching someone you love become someone you barely recognize is a terrifying experience.

If your loved one has been addicted for long, you know how his struggles can become a black hole, sucking up your family's emotional, physical, and financial resources. As you struggle to keep him alive, out of trouble, or temporarily sober, your own needs take a backseat.

But it's the mystifying nature of addiction that makes it uniquely heartbreaking. "Why can't he just stop?" is the question I hear most often from addicts' families, followed by "Why is this happening again?" and "Why doesn't anything I do seem to help?" To begin answering those questions, it's important to first gain a basic understanding of addiction and how it affects your loved one. Once you know what you're up against, you can begin learning the best ways to help your loved one and protect your own well-being.

A Chronic Disease

Traditionally, addiction has been viewed as a behavioral problem. Addicts and alcoholics were viewed as people who simply *did* something—continued drinking and using to excess—rather than people who *had* something (Sandor 2009). Over the last few decades, that view has shifted, and the scientific community now views addiction as a chronic brain disease. In August 2011, the American Society of Addiction Medicine updated its definition of addiction, describing it as a primary, chronic brain disorder, not the result of other causes, such as emotional or psychiatric problems.

It might be counterintuitive to think of addiction the same way you think of cancer or arthritis. Some people dispute addiction as a disease, in part because they think it lets addicts off the hook for their behavior. I disagree with that notion. Whether or not you embrace the idea of addiction as a disease—it *works* like one. Just like cardiovascular disease or diabetes, addiction must be treated and managed for the rest of one's life.

And just like many other chronic diseases, addiction carries a high risk of recurrence. In fact, relapse rates for drug addiction are similar to those for type 1 diabetes, hypertension, and asthma (National Institute on Drug Abuse 2008; McLellan, Lewis, O'Brien, and Kleber 2000). These are all diseases that can be managed well with lifestyle changes, and the "relapse" is failing to maintain the healthy diet, exercise, and medication regimens that will keep the physical damage done by the disease at bay.

Because of the lasting changes addiction makes to brain chemistry, your loved one isn't "cured" simply because she has stopped using the substance—even if she's been sober for years. If all of this sounds discouraging, please keep in mind that addiction is *highly* treatable. Millions of addicts who once seemed hopelessly bound to a substance have achieved lasting sobriety. Those who maintain some form of ongoing treatment stand a good chance of staying sober for the rest of their lives. (I'll discuss treatment options in chapter 5.)

Brain Chemistry Basics

What is at the root of this chronic condition? Let's look at how our brains work. When we do something positive for our body, such as eating or exercising, the brain's reward system is activated. The brain sends out naturally occurring chemicals— endorphins and dopamine among them—that make us feel good. This reward system is closely tied to emotional and subjective memories. So not only do we have a strong desire to repeat those pleasurable activities, but we also actually remember how and where the feel-good moment occurred. This explains why activities leading up to the pleasurable moment can be as addictive as the moment itself (Horvath et al. 2005–2015a).

Drugs and alcohol alter the production of those chemicals, in some cases by imitating the brain's chemical messengers, or neurotransmitters (National Institute on Drug Abuse 2012). All addictive drugs and activities release varying amounts of the neurotransmitter dopamine. However, stimulant drugs such as cocaine and methamphetamine release the most. Addictive substances and activities flood the user's system with dopamine. The resulting high or rush is a much stronger feeling of pleasure than the normal flow of dopamine provides.

While the initial feeling is great, the aftereffects are not. The departure of drugs and alcohol from the user's system can cause physical pain and depression, as the body struggles to regain its chemical balance. As a result, the motivation to restore the pleasurable feeling intensifies.

When use is repeated, the brain starts producing less of its own pleasurable and calming chemicals. As a result, the addict needs to consume more and more of the substance just to feel normal. This is when physical dependency on the drug begins. Acquiring the substance now becomes the top priority. The motivation to repeat the behavior is even stronger, even if the behaviors are harmful. This explains why your loved one will go to any lengths to obtain her drug of choice, despite the harm she causes to herself or others.

In the early stages of addiction, the pleasurable experience of the drug is what motivates a user to repeat the behavior. In later stages, the relief of withdrawal symptoms—which include both physical and emotional discomfort—perpetuates the behavior (Horvath et al. 2005–2015b).

As the reward system goes into hyperdrive, many other parts of the brain are affected. Brain functions such as learning, memory, decision making, and behavior control become less functional. This process can take anywhere from weeks to years, depending on the substance and the user.

Commonly Abused Substances

Familiarity with the most commonly abused substances can help you understand what's going on. (Note that most addicts use multiple substances.) The list below is a brief introduction to some of the most popular substances; for broader and deeper information, including emerging usage trends, visit the National Institute on Drug Abuse's website at http://www.drugabuse.gov.

- *Alcohol.* Alcohol abusers often look bloated or flushed. Though alcohol is a depressant, the loss of inhibition can produce an energizing effect. The rate of progression of alcohol addiction varies greatly; many alcoholics can function for decades. Usage patterns run the gamut from incremental drinking throughout the day to multiday binges followed by periods of abstinence.

- *Cocaine.* Most often snorted or smoked, cocaine provides a feeling of exhilaration and energy, often leading to heightened activity. It's often used to sustain energy while abusing other substances, especially alcohol. *Crack* is a less expensive, smokable form of cocaine that often provides a stronger but shorter high. Also called *coke, blow, bump.*

- *Depressants.* Ativan (lorazepam), Valium (diazepam), Klonopin (clonazepam), and Xanax (alprazolam) are commonly abused prescription benzodiazepines. Abusers of these drugs may seem sedated or drunk; they experience many of the same symptoms alcohol causes, including slurred speech and lowered inhibition. Also called *benzos, downers.*

- *Ecstasy.* Most commonly found in tablet form, the chemical compound MDMA produces an energetic, euphoric effect that often leads to extreme sociability. The term *Molly* often denotes a purer form of ecstasy, but tablets sold under either name often contain other drugs and additives. The hangover from MDMA can include acute depression. Also called *E, X, rolling.*

- *Heroin.* Heroin is usually found in powdered form; its color ranges from white to black, depending, in part, on purity. It can be smoked, snorted, or injected. Users typically experience a euphoric, relaxed state that makes them appear sleepy, introspective, and withdrawn. Pleasurable sensations diminish with repeated use. Also called *smack, horse, junk.*

- *Marijuana.* Users typically appear laid-back and relaxed, though some may exhibit paranoia and anxiety. Irritated eyes and a sweet smell are the most common signs. Abuse may lead to lethargy, disorientation, and mental-health problems. Note that the marijuana available today is, on average, much more potent than that of ten or twenty years ago. Also called *pot, weed, smoke, buds.*

- *Methamphetamine.* Most often smoked, methamphetamine can also be snorted, injected, or swallowed. The initial intense rush lasts only a few minutes. While high, meth users may be extremely talkative and exhibit manic, bizarre, or aggressive behavior. Abuse can progress quickly and cause obvious damage to skin and teeth. Also called *crystal, meth, ice, speed, Tina.*

- *Pain relievers.* Prescription pain relievers such as Vicodin (hydrocodone and acetaminophen) and Oxycontin (oxycodone) are among the most commonly abused opioids. They are usually taken in pill form. Users may exhibit drowsiness, impaired coordination, and euphoria. Also called *oxy, percs, vike.*

Contributing Factors

Of course, most people who drink or use drugs don't get caught up in the cycle of addiction. What makes some people addicts and others not? While there's no smoking gun—no single factor that determines whether someone becomes an addict—there are some common factors that make some people more susceptible than others.

Pinpointing the exact causes of an addiction is often impossible. Please keep in mind that even if you did gain that knowledge, it wouldn't cure the addiction. Nevertheless, learning more about the factors contributing to your loved one's illness can help you see it from a more objective point of view. It can also help you start thinking about the types of treatment that are most likely to help.

Most addicts have been affected by one or more of the following factors. For each factor, I've included first-hand accounts from addicts.

Mental

I used to get super-anxious in social situations. The pills made it possible for me to talk to people. It was like I was finally the chill guy I always wanted to be. But then when they wore off, I would feel even more anxious, even if I was just by myself. After a while, I started needing the pills just to get out of bed and go to work.

I never seemed to enjoy things in my life, and I thought about killing myself all the time. When I drank, even though I still felt down, I felt like I could handle things more, and at least I would forget for a little while.

Mental health is probably the number one issue underlying addiction. According to Substance Abuse and Mental Health Services (2010), 42.8 percent of adult addicts also have a co-occurring mental illness.

Many mental illnesses, including relatively minor conditions, have symptoms that foster the substance abuse that can lead to addiction. For example, depressed people may seek an escape from their misery, while anxiety sufferers may seek a calming effect. People with bipolar disorder may crave pleasure in order to stabilize their moods. Borderline personality disorder includes symptoms of impulsive behavior that can easily lead to substance abuse.

Emotional

I don't know what to do with the pain I feel inside. I discovered that when I cut myself, the feelings would go away for a little while. Then people would stare at my scars, and I felt ashamed. I would hide them. Heroin numbed my shame and pain. When I party, I don't have to feel bad.

I lost a baby during birth. It was the most emotionally painful experience of my life. I had so much hope for my baby and the future raising her. Drinking made me not think. My stress

*didn't matter anymore. I could go to sleep and not think
about it.*

Substances can provide a temporary escape from negative
emotions and painful memories. People who have not developed
adequate coping skills—for example, as a result of trauma,
neglect, or development problems—are especially likely to self-
medicate with drugs and alcohol. Even relatively minor emotional
problems can motivate someone to turn to substances for relief.

Genetic

*I have seven siblings. Even though both of my parents were
heavy drinkers, they raised us in a loving home. As far as I
can tell, only two of us are "normies" [nonaddicts]. Three
of us are in recovery programs, one is in prison on drug
charges, and two are dead.*

*No one in my adoptive family was a drinker, and still I
became an alcoholic. My disease became unmanageable
so fast. It seemed that soon after my first drink, I couldn't
get enough.*

Inherited biological traits can influence predisposition
toward addiction. To date, no "addiction gene" has been identified, but research has indicated that addiction does run in
genetic families (National Council on Alcoholism and Drug
Dependence n. d.). This doesn't mean that the disease cannot
develop without a genetic predisposition. But for those who are
genetically susceptible, the addictive cycle may kick in sooner
after initial exposure.

Physical

*I had to have back surgery, and the pain medication wasn't
helping. I thought it wouldn't hurt to double my dose till the*

pain died down. When I ran out of pills early, the pain was intolerable. The doctor gave me another prescription. This happened over and over, and eventually I needed to buy them on the street in order to tolerate the pain.

I had a hard time with the loss of my husband. It came as such a shock that one day he was here and the next day he wasn't. My doctor gave me some Xanax to get through the funeral and to calm me down for a while. Soon, I noticed that my anxiety would be so high when I didn't take them, so I took them more often, and eventually I couldn't go without them.

For many people, physical illness and chronic pain open the door to addiction. A doctor's prescription of pain-control medication becomes a justification for taking the drug. The discomfort of withdrawing from the drug can be hard to distinguish from the original pain that warranted the medication, making it much more difficult to stop.

Environmental

I never felt like I belonged anywhere. Then I met some kids at school who accepted me for who I was, and I never needed to prove anything. When we would do things that weren't right, I would get pumped up, and I felt bonded to them.

I first tried drugs because my best friend was doing it, and it seemed like she liked it so much. I understood after I tried. It became something that I got to share with her. A few months later, I started feeling like I couldn't do without it, whether she was around or not.

Environmental factors, such as where a person lives and with whom he associates, can also set the stage for addiction.

Adolescents' need for acceptance can be a powerful motivator for them to try drugs and alcohol. Stressful situations at home, school, or work can also lead to substance abuse, even in the absence of peers who are using the same substance.

Addiction vs. Substance Abuse

It can be hard to tell the difference between someone who abuses a substance and someone who has crossed the line into the chronic illness of addiction. External factors, such as whether the person is able to maintain a successful career, aren't enough to go by. Even the amount someone uses won't tell you whether that person is an addict. So what does distinguish an addict from someone who just drinks or uses too much? Most addicts share the following experiences.

Lack of Control

Most addicts try repeatedly to control their use of the substance. But once the substance is in their body, they have little or no control over how much they consume. Any intentions or promises to use the substance in moderation fall by the wayside.

It Gets Worse

Addiction is a progressive disease. As the addict's tolerance grows, so does the need for the substance. Eventually, she begins using to relieve the effects of using. More and more of the substance is required just to feel normal. The pleasure derived from using the drug may fade, but the compulsion to use it keeps growing. The substance becomes the focus of the addict's life. And if the addict resumes using the substance after a period of abstaining, the addiction soon picks up where it left off—or further along.

External Changes Don't Work

Lifestyle improvements, such as finding a less stressful job or leaving a negative relationship, might lead to a decrease in usage, but only for a while. By contrast, a nonaddict's drug or drinking problem is likely to ease up when conditions improve. Addicts tend to use in good times and bad, both to celebrate and to take solace.

Arrested Development

One commonly held belief based on clinical observation is that once people become addicted, their social and problem-solving skills stop developing normally. For example, if someone gets hooked at age sixteen, he may have a teenager's coping skills until he stops using. This interruption of the maturing process may help account for many relapses.

Hitting Bottom

The popular notion that an addict needs to bottom out completely before she can begin to recover is dangerous. If someone you cared for had heart disease, would you wait until she had a heart attack to start addressing the problem? Growing awareness of addiction has led many addicts and alcoholics to get treatment in the earliest stages of the disease, often saving themselves and their families decades of suffering. Whether there is addiction or chronic substance abuse present, intervention when there is indication of a problem is the right decision.

An Addiction Journal

As a family member or friend of an addict, you have a more objective lens through which to view the addiction than the addict has. But that's only if you can step away from the situation and see it clearly. Starting a dedicated journal will help you do just that.

Use your journal to complete the exercises at the end of each chapter—and also to record your thoughts and feelings whenever the mood strikes you, whether you're feeling overwhelmed and scared or you just want to celebrate good news. I also recommend setting aside a short period for writing at the same time every day. Writing for even a few minutes a day—without worrying about how much sense you're making or what others might think if they read it—can have a surprisingly calming effect. It's a great way to keep your own experience from getting swept up into the chaos the addiction may bring.

Exercise 1 takes a slightly different angle toward that same goal. It's designed to give you practice expressing observations without anger or judgment. It will serve as a first step toward discussing the problem effectively with your loved one and other family members.

Exercise 1: Just the Facts

As you answer the questions below, try to avoid opinions, judgments, generalizations, and exaggerations. For example, "She hangs out with shady characters all the time" includes both a judgment (*shady*) and an exaggeration (*all the time*). By contrast, "She socializes with people I don't trust two or three nights a week" contains only observations.

- Has your loved one been diagnosed with a mental health problem, or do you suspect she might have one? What are the symptoms?

- What is your loved one's emotional state like? Have there been incidents that were emotionally stressful? Think of recent events as well as those in the past.

- Has your loved one faced any physical challenges?

- Does drug or alcohol abuse run in the family? Name all relatives who have or who you suspect might have a substance addiction.

- Describe the environment of your loved one, including home and work life.

- Make a list of things that have been done or said—either by the addicted person or by others—regarding the substance abuse that concern you. Be as specific as possible. If you can remember dates, record those as well. And don't limit yourself to recent interactions—go as far back as you need to.

- Describe a time when you felt your loved one was not yet addicted. Be as specific as possible, describing, without judgment, his personality, behavior, likes and dislikes, and so forth. Now contrast that with his current behavior.

- What substance or substances do you think are being abused? How often and how much? Cite specific evidence if possible. If you don't know, write "I don't know."

- What specific actions have been taken to change your loved one's behavior relating to the substance or substances? For example, has she tried abstaining or seeking treatment? What have been the results of these attempts?

Well done! Taking an unflinching look at the struggles is a major accomplishment. As you wrote your answers, how did you feel? Even though you described things as objectively as possible, I'm guessing that you felt plenty of emotion. The intent of this exercise is not to help you avoid emotion but to help you recognize that you can feel scared, angry, guilty, or confused without letting those emotions cloud your observations. Keep your answers handy; we'll need them as we move into positive action.

What Now?

I've focused on addicts and addiction in this chapter because they're the source of so much despair and confusion. But ultimately, this book isn't about the addict in your life. It's about you.

Addiction is not your fault. It's a chronic illness with origins that may never become perfectly clear. I also hope you've begun to mentally separate the addiction from the person you love. Both of these concepts will help you maintain a clear perspective as you move into action.

In the next chapter, we'll take a closer look at addictive behavior—and how it can intertwine with your own—as a way to prepare you to make changes that will help you protect yourself while helping your loved one.

CHAPTER 2

Addicts' Behavior— and Your Own

My once-thoughtful brother now didn't seem to care about anything or anyone. He would regularly just disappear. I felt an instinctive need to go look for him. He was a grown man living on his own, yet I chased him around, rescuing him from places I would never otherwise risk going. I picked him up from seedy motels, scolding the front desk clerk for selling him alcohol. I picked him up from jail. And while I was driving him to detox facilities, he'd threaten to throw himself from the moving car if I didn't stop to buy him alcohol.

Our parents provided for his treatments to the point of financial sacrifice. We all re-prioritized our lives to take care of him. I remember my intense range of emotions: rage, sadness, grief, and paralyzing confusion. Yet he disregarded all the chaos he had created and continued to drink, as if his actions had no effect on us. There was no logic to his behavior. I didn't understand why he wouldn't just stop.

When you have an addicted loved one, it can sometimes feel like nothing you do makes a difference. That impression is false. While you can't fix her addiction, you can guide her toward getting the help she needs. In order to do that, however, you must first understand her behavior—and how it can affect your own.

Nonaddicts have a hard time grasping how much power an addiction holds over an addict. Most people would be shocked by the way an entire existence can be directed toward getting drunk or high. To live as an addict, you may connive and cheat, lie and steal—whatever it takes—to feed your disease.

Imagine going without food for a prolonged period. After a while, the lack of nourishment would begin to affect your actions and your mood. You might make mistakes or exercise poor judgment. Before long, your hunger would take precedence. We'd all like to think that we'd behave honorably in the face of hunger, but it's easy to believe that with a full belly. If you had to manipulate someone or distort the truth or even steal in order to feed yourself, at some point, you probably would.

An addict's pursuit of alcohol or drugs works in a similar way. Like hunger, being addicted is not a deliberate state. It is biological in nature. An untreated addict has no more control of his or her actions than you might if you were starving. In the grip of an addiction, your loved one's previously held standards and principles no longer apply.

That's true even for addicts who might be referred to as "functional"—those who maintain their jobs, pay their bills, and get by on a daily basis. These addicts have as active and debilitating a disease as those whose lives are more obviously dominated by substance abuse. "Functional" addicts conceal their disease in the false belief that they still have their lives under control. But under the surface, they are slaves to the addiction. Keeping up appearances becomes just another symptom of the disease.

Until you understand what drives an addict's behavior and thinking, your attempts to help will likely have little effect—and they may even help the addiction thrive. This chapter explores how addicts live and think and how family and friends can be manipulated and deceived in the addicts' quest to continue using their substance of choice. By the end of the chapter, you'll understand how their addictive behavior affects your efforts to help them. Seeing the behavior more clearly is a critical step toward providing assistance that actually helps—and protecting yourself and your family.

When you think of an addict's behavior, the first thing that comes to mind might be how he acts when he's drunk or high—reckless, careless, unpredictable. But the truly insidious part of addiction is how it affects your loved one when he's *not* intoxicated. Even when he isn't high or drunk, the addiction is working behind the scenes to ensure its survival. That means making sure the addict can get more of the substance—by any means necessary—and shutting down any factors that could threaten his continuing use.

The Addictive Thought Process

Addictive thinking patterns are different from normal thought processes. While you or I might consider long-term consequences and adjust our behavior accordingly, an addict is incapable of doing so.

The diagrams below depict how an active addict's thought process differs from a nonaddict's. At the center of an addict's thought process is the substance she is seeking. Everything else—including attention to herself—revolves around the need for that substance.

In a normal, healthy thought process, the central focus is the individual self. This doesn't mean self-centeredness, but the everyday self-care that we all need to function in society and in our own lives. Everything else, including whether we choose to indulge in a drink or two, revolves around that central focus.

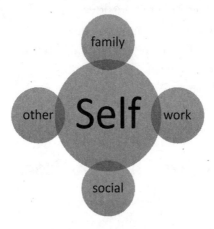

The addicts' focus on attaining the high is so strong that they become completely absorbed in their quest. As we learned in chapter 1, the seeking out of the substance becomes a ritual experience that enhances the pleasure of the end result.

This all-consuming drive leads to irrational decision making. Addicts will make impulsive decisions without thinking of long-term consequences or considering whom they might hurt in the process.

Addicts tend to focus on what is being done *to* them, not *by* them. The addict will attribute the consequences of the addiction—broken relationships, financial problems, legal trouble—not to the addiction, but to the world and the people in it. An addict will say, "My boss is unreasonable." "My girlfriend can't be trusted." "Everyone's out to get me!" Have you heard your loved one make these statements? It's because he's come to believe these exaggerations as truths, and he is voicing them to try to make you believe them too. Moreover, this kind of distorted thinking serves an important purpose: to justify continued use of the substance.

The Addict's Internal Conflict

What's behind an addict's irrational, self-destructive behavior? My clients frequently tell me that being an addict is like having two different people inside of them. Consider these statements:

> When the obsession kicks in, there is no stopping it. It is like I am two people, and the bad one always wins. It is horrible being an addict. When the thought occurs to me to use, I tell the world to kiss off. I usually do it without even hesitating.

> I know, when I pick up my first drink of the day, what the outcome is going to be. I have been told numerous times that if I don't stop, I will die. For some reason, something inside me refuses to believe this, and I believe that I am supposed to suffer till the day I die.

These addicts' explanations of their own experiences point us toward the key to understanding their behavior. Addicts feel like they're split because they are—they're driven by their addiction, which wants only to continue using the substance, no matter what. At the same time, they may also be able to see, at least occasionally, the damage their addiction is doing, but they still feel unable to stop.

Some people have difficulty accepting this view of the addict, thinking it lets them off the hook for their own behavior—or that it sounds too much like some kind of mystical possession. I understand these reservations, but from a practical point of view, approaching it on these terms gives you your best chance of influencing your loved one in a positive direction.

Keeping this internal split in mind will also help you overcome the guilt and fear that can leave you feeling paralyzed and powerless. Saying no to someone who is obviously suffering is agonizing. But saying no to your loved one's *addiction* can be gratifying and empowering. When you truly grasp that you're fighting the addiction, not your addicted loved one, it becomes much easier to set boundaries, make tough decisions, and know when it's best to take a step back from the situation. You'll become more able to truly help and to avoid inadvertently feeding the addiction.

Recognizing Addiction's Top Strategies

An addiction's only purpose is to feed itself. To do so, it uses a wide array of strategies, often hijacking the addict's intelligence, skills, and relationships. Once you recognize these strategies for what they are, they become much easier to deal with—and neutralize.

Denial

Addicts experience many different levels of denial, ranging from underreporting the amount they drink or use drugs to denying—even to themselves—that they have a problem. When I interview an alcoholic for the first time, I always ask how many drinks he consumes daily. Most will minimize in an attempt to make their problem not look so bad, even to the therapist they are seeing for help. Assume that the amount of substance use reported by your loved one is lower than the actual amount. In most cases, the downplayed amount is what the addict would consider to be an acceptable level. Minimizing the amount they drink or use may be an effort to avoid embarrassment or shame. But from the addiction's point of view, it's also a way to minimize others' concerns, which could lead to confrontation—and maybe eventually to sobriety.

When confronted about her drinking or drug use, the addict may shift the attention to someone else who's at a more advanced stage of addiction, saying, "Now *he's* an addict." In some cases, such people may be kept around for exactly this purpose—to serve as reassurance for the addict that her own problem isn't so serious. Similarly, she may claim that you and other family members are irrational about her use, pointing out that those outside the family have no concern about it (usually pointing to people who don't have a front-row seat on the addiction).

Your loved one may also cite as evidence his continuing career, relationship, and health, seizing upon any remaining positive element to prove that everything's okay.

Many addicted people really do believe that they can stop whenever they want to. And even if they *are* aware, on some level, that the problem has reached uncontrollable levels, they're not willing to confront that reality, due to the incredible effort resolving it would require.

From the addict's viewpoint, there can be a fine line between abuse and addiction. They will often fight to maintain the notion that they can "just stop," using it to argue that they are not addicted and don't need treatment. By attempting to stop in the short term, they try to persuade themselves and others that they have control of their substance use and are okay. Most will simply attempt to hide it better or will justify the return to use.

Justification

Your loved one may offer a multitude of reasons for her drinking or using, as well as the resulting behavior. There may be citations about the stresses of her life and how the substance helps her "blow off steam," "unwind," "chill," or "relax."

Addicts may be aware that their behavior has become unacceptable—and they may even acknowledge it at times. But any thoughts that threaten to interfere with getting their drug of choice are explained away before long. For example, if an addict takes someone's necklace to pawn for drug money, he may tell himself that the victim hadn't worn it in years and will probably never even notice that it's gone. (And besides, he'll buy it back as soon as he gets a little money.) At some level, addicts know the behavior is wrong, but guilt doesn't really kick in until the high is gone—at which point it serves as more motivation to get high again.

The rationalization is often that no one is getting hurt by the addict's behavior—especially if she's using her own money to feed her disease. The truth is that she may be causing sleepless nights for everyone who cares about her.

Another common form of justifying is exceptionalism. The addict recognizes that his behavior is dangerous and would generally be unacceptable for most people, but he thinks the rules somehow don't apply to him. (In Alcoholics Anonymous, this belief is sometimes referred to as "terminal uniqueness.") You can see how useful this concept is for an addiction, since it serves as a green light for virtually any behavior. No matter how bad the consequences or how hopeless the situation, the addict can always think, "Well, that may be true for everyone else, but I'm different."

Deception

However honest your loved one was before the addiction took hold, once she becomes an addict, deception will likely become frequent and pervasive. After all, to be honest about her life would be to alert others that her addiction is a dangerous force that needs to be stopped.

Many addicts can keep it together in all aspects of their lives for a while. Some can even hide their use from the people who see them all day, every day. Sadly, family members tend to be the easiest to deceive, due to the level of trust inherent in most family units—and their desire not to believe the reality.

To protect their addiction, addicts also commonly lie to employers, friends, and even the professionals they've hired to help them—sometimes for years. (I'll address this problem in chapter 3.)

Manipulation

Of all the tools addiction uses to protect itself, its favorite might be *you*. Many addicts become master manipulators, turning the people in their lives into unknowing guardians of their addiction. If you were to ask just about any addict in rehab, she could tell you who among the people she knows is the most easily manipulated person and who is the control freak. Addicts will tell you whom they can make cry most easily and whom they cannot approach at all. If you know an addict or care for one, you are predestined for a role in the play. This doesn't mean that the addict doesn't love you. It means that the addiction is willing to protect itself by any means necessary. If there's a way your personality, values, fears, skills, or hopes can be used toward that end, the addiction will eventually seek to exploit it.

Sadly, the most commonly exploited quality is love. The more you care for someone, the more susceptible you'll be to inadvertently protecting the addiction. Knowing how much we want to see them get better, addicts will provide glimpses of progress in order to provide cover for their continued use. They seem to know instinctively just when to act like they're finally ready to get help—and they may even convince themselves briefly that they are.

Manipulation may take many other forms. For example, an addict may exploit your dislike of another person, perhaps blaming that person for the problems his addiction has created. Or he might divert attention away from the addiction by creating drama—picking a fight with someone, setting two people against each other, or spreading a rumor.

Negotiation might seem like the opposite of manipulation. After all, it involves finding middle ground between two opposing parties. But when you're dealing with an addiction, all negotiation is a form of manipulation—an attempt to turn a one-sided issue into an exchange. An example could be "Let's just have a good time through the holidays, and I'll quit when they are over," or "If you buy me a bottle, I will go to that event with you." Making a deal places the addict's behavior in a circumstantial context, as though it depended on external conditions. As we learned in chapter 1, that's not how addiction works. If an addict were capable of exchanging his addiction for some material reward, he would have done so by now.

Manipulation can be a powerful force, but it has one glaring weakness: it doesn't work without some unconscious participation from the person being manipulated. By recognizing manipulation and consciously refusing to take part, you can neutralize one of addiction's most effective strategies.

Are You Enabling the Addiction?

In some cases, addicts hardly need to lift a finger to enlist others in protecting their disease. These other people may also be justifying or minimizing the addicts' behavior. *Enabling* describes dysfunctional behavior that shields the addict from the negative effects of his addictive behavior.

For example, a woman did her husband's reports for work because he was too intoxicated to do them himself. She didn't want him to get fired. But by doing his work, she ensured there would be no consequences for him. She bore the brunt of the responsibility and the stress, and he continued to drink.

Enabling behaviors are usually motivated by well-meaning intentions. Naturally, you want to help. You want her to be able to keep her job, take care of her children, pay her bills, and stay out of legal trouble. By easing some of the stress of her life, you might think you'll decrease her motivation to drink or use. The difficult truth is that if this person is addicted, that kind of cause-and-effect relationship no longer applies. As we learned in chapter 1, circumstantial improvements won't have any lasting effect on an addiction. Before long, the same or worse consequences will return.

The temporary benefits of helping your loved one, including any sense of gratification you get from helping, come at a high price. You've helped him avoid the one factor that motivates addicts to stop using more than any other: pain.

In some cases, it does become necessary to protect an addicted person from harm, even if you might also be shielding her from the addiction's consequences. I'll address some of these special circumstances—and discuss the most effective forms of help you can provide—in the section "Assessing Danger" in chapter 4.

Putting an end to enabling doesn't have to mean turning your back on someone you love. It does mean being careful that any help you provide is helping the person, not her addiction. Telling the difference between those two can be difficult, and I'll walk you through that process in chapter 4, in the section "When an Addict Asks for Help." For now, ask yourself the following questions about your behavior:

- Do I make excuses for my loved one? For example, "He's not drunk; he's just tired" or "He works so hard and needs a break."

- Do I take over my loved one's responsibilities, such as paying bills or helping with work projects or childcare?

- Have I lent or given money to my loved one for "emergencies"?

- Do I micromanage my loved one, for example, by escorting her to appointments to ensure that she goes or checking her cell phone for messages?

All of these enabling behaviors shift the responsibility from your loved one to you. That's an enormous stress that you don't need to bear. And assuming responsibility can foster the inaccurate notion that you can fix your loved one, which can only lead to heartbreak and years of wasted energy.

Once you've embraced the idea that you're dealing with the addiction, not the person you love, you can start making more effective choices about the help you provide. Over time, you'll move from a vague sense that you're never doing enough to a clear conviction that you are doing what you can.

Enabling Doesn't Work

You may believe that you alone can save the addict in your life. You might think, "Without me to take care of everything, my loved one will die." This faulty view of what's happening sets you up for heartache and a feeling of continuous failure. You do have a role to play, but you need to understand and accept its limits.

Coming to this understanding is painful. The instinct to help runs deep; ignoring it or acting against it can seem unnatural, immoral, and heartless. That's why it's important to regularly remind yourself why enabling doesn't work. The following three points about enabling are worth revisiting whenever you find yourself tempted to keep your loved one out of trouble:

- **It delays consequences.** Shielding the addict from the real wreckage of his behavior helps maintain the illusion that things aren't as bad as they are. That makes it easier for him to continue using, which will soon bring additional—and usually worse—consequences.

- **It transfers responsibility.** Establishing a pattern of rescuing moves responsibility away from the only person who has the power to change the situation: the addict herself. That's an ideal situation for an addiction, which relies on its host to be as passive as possible.

- **It doesn't work.** The substance abuse might have initially been influenced by external factors, but if your loved one has crossed the line into addiction, improving those conditions won't have a lasting effect.

Changing your behavior isn't easy. When I refused to help my brother that night he called me from a park bench, after years of relapse and deception, it was one of the most painful things I'd ever experienced. But I see now that it was also necessary, for both of us. Every time I'd rescued him over the years, I'd been fooling myself. For the momentary good feeling of bailing him out or protecting him, I was also helping him delay the process that finally led to his sobriety. I was playing a part in his addiction's game, rather than standing up to it.

Keeping Responsibility Where It Belongs

We've learned how an addiction can take control of an addict's thinking and behavior. This process *doesn't* mean that the addict should be absolved of responsibility for her substance abuse and all the wreckage it creates. The responsibility still lies with the addict for a very practical reason: *only* the addict can decide to change, and *only* the addict can make it happen.

Once you accept this, the complexities involved in getting the necessary care become much simpler. If the addict wants to get better, he will take the steps necessary toward accomplishing that goal. This does not mean that it will be accomplished the first or even the tenth time. It does mean that there is a learning process and an internal struggle that the addict will need to address. The road to achieving that may not be smooth. There is no such thing as not being capable of recovering, of being too sick. If your loved one is not getting better, chances are that something is holding him back. Often, addicts will have hidden reservations about living without their drug. Sometimes this can be fear; sometimes it can be an activity or a relationship that includes the use of substances; sometimes it can just be the unknown of what life will be like when they stop using.

Get in Addiction's Head

Another way to understand how addicts think is by getting a feel for how the addiction "thinks." If you can put yourself in the addiction's shoes, so to speak, you can also see how your responses can help or hinder recovery.

Exercise 2: Be the Addiction

Number a page of your journal 1 through 10, leaving a few lines for each number. On the first line of each item, write something you've done in response to the addiction. Keep the descriptions short and simple. For example, "Asked him how much he was drinking," "Kicked him out of the house," "Lent him rent money," "Drove him to NA meeting," "Gave him my car when he totaled his," "Lied to his employer to cover for him," or "Refused to let him stay here when he was using." If you can't think of ten actions you've done, use actions taken by other family members.

Next, imagine yourself as the addiction—*not your loved one, but the disease that lives inside of him.* Remember: as an addiction, all you care about is that the addict continues to use. Underneath each action listed, describe the way you, as an addiction, would respond to it. Are you happy about the action? Do you feel threatened by it? Why? What can you do in response? For example: "If she's asking me how much I'm drinking, she must not know! I'll just lie and say I'm drinking only on the weekends. It's none of her business anyway." "I didn't like being kicked out of the house—not one bit." "I hate going to NA meetings! If she wouldn't drive me there, I certainly wouldn't go. When I'm there, I feel threatened." "Yes! Now that I have a car again, it'll be so much easier to drink whenever and wherever I want and still go to work—not that I care about work, but I have to keep up appearances. And it's nice to know that if I wreck something else, I can go to her for help!" And so on.

When you're done with the exercise, read through all your responses. Take special note of actions that were either strongly negative or strongly positive for the addiction. If you aren't sure about some of the addiction's responses, that's perfectly understandable. For example, you might have lied to his employer so your loved one wouldn't lose his job—a good thing, right? But if you look at the addiction's response—"Now that I've got a good excuse for my boss, I can use my next paycheck to buy more drugs and really celebrate!"—you can see how this action, however well intentioned, greatly benefits the addiction. Knowing the difference between genuinely helping the person and protecting the addiction is not always easy. Referring back to this exercise when you are unsure can help clarify the situation.

What Now?

In this chapter, we've delved into how addicts live and think, and we've explored how an addiction will do whatever it can to ensure its own survival, manipulating you and anyone else to ensure the addict's continued use. You've also learned how to recognize enabling behaviors—forms of help that mean well but often end up serving the addiction, not the person underneath.

It might not feel like it, but opting out of manipulation and enabling is a great step toward helping. And it's only the beginning of what you can do. In the next chapter, I'll guide you into action. You'll learn the best ways to communicate with an addict—what works and what doesn't—and how to talk with others about the addiction.

CHAPTER 3

Communication

After many long and emotional conversations about all the things he knew he had to do to stay sober—go to meetings, steer clear of bars, get rid of his drug dealer's number, reach out for help if he was struggling—my brother relapsed again. All the lecturing, talking, and pleading over the years had amounted to nothing. We were back at square one. I couldn't understand how all of our heartfelt conversations could once again be pushed aside.

I tried a different approach. With my mother and a friend who was a drug counselor, I went to his home to talk to him and hopefully get him to commit to treatment—again. Instead of making that commitment, my brother turned the focus onto me. "I didn't ask for your help; I don't need your help; I don't want your help. Why don't you look at your own life instead of mine?" The communication ceased.

It was the most honest thing he'd said to me in years. And he was right. I had been so focused on how to fix him and his situation that I hadn't realized how strongly my own codependency issues were at work. The conversation hadn't yielded the result I wanted, but it did communicate a startling truth. Instead of the broken record of telling him what he should do, followed by him agreeing to do it—and then eventually not doing it—I should have focused on what I needed to do to take care of myself. Only after I began to do that did my communication make a difference for either of us.

If you've been dealing with an addicted loved one for a while, you know how frustrating communicating with her can be: the same arguments, debates, apologies, and promises, over and over, all leading nowhere. Even when it seems like you've gotten through to her, her later actions say otherwise. You spend sleepless nights ruminating about past conversations and planning future ones, puzzling over the magic combination of words that will finally get her to quit.

You won't find it. Sadly, you can't talk your loved one into getting sober. As we've learned, addictions don't work that way. But you can start building a healthier relationship, whether she accepts help or not. In this chapter, I'll show you how to change your communication habits in ways that stop supporting the addiction and start supporting recovery. Your loved one will learn that you care, that you're willing to provide the right kind of help, and that you can't be manipulated.

Also, when you communicate in ways that reinforce the reality and significance of your experience, your own outlook will begin to change. You'll stop going in circles and start seeing a path out of the confusion.

What Doesn't Work

The unconscious communication patterns you've developed with your loved one likely took root before the addiction did. As a result, they're not a good fit for the present reality, which is dominated by the addiction. And even if your loved one has been addicted for as long as you've known him, the way you communicate likely evolved in a way that accommodates the addiction rather than challenging it. Patterns that work fine in your other relationships backfire when you're trying to talk to an addict. To protect your well-being and influence your loved one in a positive direction, you must change how you communicate.

This mismatch between old patterns and the new reality yields fruitless results. Attempts at talking to addicts about the problem tend to create ever-deepening ruts. Here are some of the most common types of statements addicts hear from family and friends:

- *Pleading:* "Can't you see what you're doing to yourself? Please just stop."

- *Demanding:* "You need to get ahold of yourself."

- *Blaming:* "You're making my life a living hell."

- *Threatening:* "If you keep using, I'll never speak to you again."

- *Judging:* "Do you really think you're being a good mother?"

- *Berating:* "How could you do this to us?"

- *Exaggerating:* "You never show up when you say you will."

One unfortunate truth about all of these statements is that they're *hopeful.* That might sound like a strange description for such wounded, angry statements, but underneath the frustration is the belief that, by using the right combination of logic, shame, and anger, you can persuade the addict to change his ways. In effect, your hope for change can serve to help preserve the status quo. Of course, this doesn't mean you should give up hope! But by changing your communication habits, you can give your hope a better chance of becoming reality.

If you were talking to a nonaddict, any of the above statements would stand a chance of having the desired effect. Embarrassment, shame, guilt, or fear might motivate a person with a mere substance problem to modify her behavior. But as we've learned, addicts *can't* control their behavior involving alcohol and drugs. That's why none of the statements can have any lasting effect. (And addicts have an automatic response to all that guilt and shame: using more of their preferred substance as soon as possible.)

By focusing on the addict's behavior, those statements also shift attention away from the underlying problem: the addiction. The chronic disease that fuels so much suffering stays safely tucked away while you argue about its symptoms. When you just talk about his symptomatic behavior—getting to work late, not paying bills on time, breaking a promise—you are unwittingly playing along. It may feel like you're directly attacking the addiction, but you're never actually threatening it. When you communicate, do your best to keep the topic on the addiction. The exercise at the end of this chapter will help you distinguish between a statement about the addiction and one about its symptoms.

Finally, each of the above statements places the addict at the center of your world. The addict is treated as though she can control not only her own behavior but also *your* well-being. These twin delusions can back you into a painful, dangerous corner. If that's where you find yourself now, learning better ways of communicating can help you escape.

Ending the Debate

So if you can't talk your loved one into quitting, what *can* you do? Plenty. By changing your communication habits, you can transform your relationship into one that offers unconditional love for the addict, supports genuine attempts at recovery, and refuses to cooperate with addiction. Your first step is opting out of unproductive conversations.

The Problem with Arguments

Most family relationships involve plenty of back-and-forth. People who care deeply about each other negotiate, compromise, and argue. In a healthy relationship, these can all be ways to maintain balance and accommodate each person's needs. When one person is in the grip of an addiction, however, these checks and balances stop working. Rather than sparking change, negotiations provide cover for the worsening addiction.

While the nonaddict is still treating the argument as part of a relationship with her loved one, in reality, it functions much more like a relationship with the addiction. And you can't "hash things out" with an addiction, which only cares about you to the extent that you can help it survive.

The Symptoms Are Not the Problem

What does all this sound like? Let's eavesdrop on a typical exchange between a woman and her alcoholic husband.

Elisa: "When you tried to drive after you'd been drinking, I was scared, because I thought you might hurt yourself or someone else."

Elisa does a good job of reporting her own experience and avoiding judgmental or subjective evaluations (as you did in exercise 1).

Jon: "I was barely buzzed—I was fine to drive."

Jon shifts the focus away from Elisa's fear by minimizing the problem.

Elisa: "Are you crazy? You were smashed!"

Elisa takes the bait by defending her position with an emotional judgment about his behavior.

From here on, the conversation has very little chance of yielding productive results. While it might seem like Jon and Elisa are in direct conflict, at a more fundamental level, they're now playing on the same team. They're both focusing on a subjective evaluation of how intoxicated he was. What both of them miss is that his drunkenness is just a symptom of the problem, not the problem itself: the chronic disease of addiction, which will cause more and more suffering until Jon gets treatment.

The only winner of this kind of debate is his addiction. As long as the conversation is about Jon's symptoms, it reinforces the delusion that the problem can be solved on an external level. It's like trying to cure emphysema by coughing less—or in Elisa's case, by persuading Jon to drink less.

Standing By Your Experience

Some of the most effective conversations you can have with an addict are distinguished by what you *don't* say. Let's imagine a more productive ending to Elisa and Jon's exchange:

Jon: "I was barely buzzed! I was fine to drive."

Elisa: "I heard you slurring your words and saw you stumble. But I'm not going to debate you. The point is that I was scared."

Here, instead of judging or arguing about her husband's behavior, Elisa stands by her own experience and explicitly declines to enter a debate about his symptoms. The exchange might seem anticlimactic, because she hasn't convinced Jon of anything, confronted the addiction directly, or even asked him to get help. But she's reinforced to herself and (possibly) to Jon that her own needs matter, and she's refused to participate in the "how drunk was Jon" shell game. This is the kind of exchange— simple, clear, undramatic—upon which she can begin building a healthier relationship with herself and with him.

Of course, there's a lot more Elisa could have said to Jon, and there's a lot more you can say to your loved one. Doing so effectively comes naturally to almost no one. It doesn't require you to memorize and recite some kind of script, but it does require learning and implementing some guiding principles.

How to Talk to Your Loved One

You might have heard that you can't help an addict until he bottoms out and seeks help on his own. This notion is based on an undeniable truth: that ultimately, only the addict can decide to accept help. But the idea that there's nothing you can do is a dangerous myth. People who care about addicts can—and do—influence them toward getting help every day.

Once you start thinking of the addicted condition the same way you think of other chronic diseases, it can be difficult to keep your concerns to yourself. If you do it skillfully, it can serve to increase your own peace of mind whether or not your loved one responds in an encouraging way.

Addiction relies on shadows and secrets. Clear, honest communication drags it into daylight. By calmly stating your experience and concerns, you can avoid the drama that distracts attention from the real problem. But you don't have to hide your emotions to make your point. On the contrary: healthier communication requires you to stay in touch with what you're feeling and how you're affected by your loved one's behavior.

There's no simple formula for talking to an addict, but there are guiding principles that can lead the conversation in the right direction. To call attention to the sometimes subtle differences between effective and ineffective approaches, I've paired the following list into dos and don'ts.

Do be truthful: The plain truth of your experience is one of the most loving gifts you can give an addict. She may not be ready or able to accept it, but minimizing or exaggerating your feelings and observations only supports the fictionalized world the addiction has built for itself.

...but don't vent: Talking *about* your feelings is different from taking them out on your loved one or blaming her for your feelings. Accusations and outbursts invite argument, drawing attention away from the progressive illness. Shaming will drive the addict

directly to the preferred substance. "I'm worried that things will just get worse if you don't get help" is a better message than "Just *look* at yourself!" A support group or therapist can provide a safer forum for voicing anger. (More on these options in chapter 9.)

Do ask your loved one to consider getting help: For most addicts, accepting help is a less unthinkable concept than living without their substance. The difference might sound trivial to you, but messages that immediately contradict the addiction's survival aren't likely to be heard. Ask only for the willingness to take a first step toward change.

...but don't ask him to quit using: This request or demand or plea, as reasonable as it seems to you, makes about as much sense to many addicts as "stop breathing." And if your request *does* make sense to your loved one, it supports the delusion that the addiction is a behavioral problem he can control. An observation such as "I know this is hard. It seems to me like you can't 'just quit,' " will be more productive.

Do identify specific forms of help: A vague plan to seek help if and when things get worse only buys time for the addiction, guaranteeing that things *will* get worse. Instead, line up concrete forms of potential help. For example, identify a nearby rehabilitation center that has an opening or find a recovering addict in your social circle who is willing to talk to your loved one.

...but don't hound your loved one about it: Once you've let your loved one know how you're willing to help, there's no need to continually repeat the offer. Doing so supports the idea that you're taking responsibility for him and monitoring or managing his condition. This plays right into the addiction's hands, since ultimately your loved one is the only one who can decide to accept help. "My coworker's brother, Keith, says he'll give you a call this week. He's the one I told you about last week who's eleven years sober. He's looking forward to talking to you" is a

better message than "When are you going to call Keith? I told you about him a week ago, and you still haven't contacted him!"

Do listen: Avoiding debate doesn't mean you should deliver a speech and walk away. By listening patiently, without jumping in to provide your views, you give your loved one a chance to hear herself. Addictive thinking makes much more sense within the safety of an addict's mind than it does out loud. Listening compassionately to someone who is suffering doesn't mean you condone her thinking. The more you practice this skill, the more you'll be able to mentally separate the person you love from the addiction. You'll also make it easier for your loved one to open up to you again.

...but don't advise: The bad decisions and lies and negative influences in your loved one's life may seem so obvious to you that it's difficult not to play therapist or life coach. But any advice you give—breaking up with someone, going back to school, exercising more—just takes pressure off the real problem: the addiction. It also needlessly adds to your emotional workload. You might say, "I hear what you're saying about being stressed out and unhappy at work and about how lonely you feel sometimes. That must be very hard," instead of, "If you stopped hanging out with your loser friends and put more effort into looking for a new job, you'd be so much happier, and we could stop arguing!"

Do acknowledge positive signs: Addiction is lonely and miserable. In most cases, addicts eventually lose sight of the possibility of feeling good without their substance of choice. Signs that your loved one is beginning to recognize the seriousness of the problem, genuinely trying to stop, or seeking help should be acknowledged and encouraged.

...but be careful with praise: Even an innocuous-sounding statement like "You made my day!" can reinforce the notion that your well-being is dependent on the addict's behavior. Instead, frame

praise in terms of your own experience and save your accolades for actions, not promises or plans. "When I heard you went to a meeting, I felt hopeful" is a better message than "It made me so proud when you said you wouldn't drink at your sister's wedding!"

Do express love: One way to reinforce the distinction between the addict and the addiction is to express unconditional love for the person while refusing to do anything that will support the addiction. Frequently remind her that you love and support *her*. By doing so, you also remind yourself, which can keep you from falling too far into anger or resentment.

...but don't soothe: When your loved one is suffering after the latest calamity his addiction has caused, it can be very tempting to comfort him with statements like "You're going to be all right" or "Things aren't so bad." A more loving thing to say would be, "That sounds awful. From what I understand, addiction only gets worse." It's not only possible but also essential to express care without minimizing what's going on.

Do choose a good time: Many addicts are most willing to discuss addiction when they're reeling from its effects, such as during a bad hangover or after an embarrassing or frightening episode. But note that others may be at their most defensive in such moments, when their denial is working overtime to reframe what just happened. If she expresses doubts about her substance use or behavior, be sure to *listen* and acknowledge that you've heard her before expressing yourself.

...but don't wait for the perfect moment: Keep in mind that your loved one's illness is progressive. Just about anytime your loved one isn't intoxicated or potentially violent is fine. In general, it's best not to schedule a very important talk, which just gives the addiction time to get its defenses lined up.

The most important thing about these principles is that they don't depend on the addict's response to be successful. Whether she's receptive or not, they'll help you protect your well-being. Even if she doesn't seem to be listening, your messages might plant seeds that will germinate later. And as we'll see in the chapters ahead, there's plenty more you can do, both on your own and with the help of others.

Communicating with Others

Addiction thrives on isolation—not only the addict's secret life but also the private suffering of the people who care about him. In many cases, a family member of an addict has no idea that other people (sometimes even a spouse, sibling, or child) have also been deeply affected by the addiction. Sharing stories with one another about your experiences can validate the pain and confusion of dealing with an addict.

Privacy vs. Urgency

If you feel hesitant to talk about your experiences out of consideration for privacy or reputation, take a close look at your motives. Would you be sharing partly out of a desire to punish, embarrass, or humiliate the addict? Or would you be sharing it only out of concern for everyone involved? Can the person you'd be sharing it with be trusted with the information?

If you're uncomfortable with your answers to these questions, don't take that as a sign to keep quiet about the problem. A professional therapist can provide the safe audience you need and more. (I'll discuss therapy options in chapter 9.)

A family's recovery from addiction is rarely a smooth, harmonious process. Sharing your experience might lead to some conflict. When you have doubts about sharing your concerns, ask yourself if you'd stay quiet about your loved one's cancer if talking about it could accelerate the treatment process. As long as you're speaking only for yourself and are motivated by care and concern, you're moving in the right direction. Also keep in mind that other family members might be waiting for someone to break the silence.

Talking with members of your family might lead to a group effort to communicate with the addict about his addiction, a topic I'll cover in the next chapter. But even if it doesn't, getting together to talk can lay the foundation for a lifetime of recovery for your family.

Finding Other Allies

A recovering addict can be a powerful resource for you and your family. Even if you don't think you know one, ask around; you probably do. If you don't find one among your immediate friends, you might find that a close friend is related to one. Sober addicts can help you better understand the process of addiction and recovery.

Often a recovering addict may serve as a powerful example. Many addicts, reciting the mantra "you just don't get it," will tune out anything a nonaddict says about substance abuse and addiction. They tend to be much more willing to listen to—and speak honestly with—someone who's been there. Most recovering addicts will gladly share their experience; helping others recover is a basic tenet of 12-step programs like Alcoholics Anonymous and Narcotics Anonymous.

Keep in mind that no one person has all the answers about sobriety, no matter how long it's been since her last drink or drug. But by sharing what worked for them, recovering addicts can provide living proof that life without their substance is possible.

Friends of Addiction

Sadly, addictions have allies, too. In many cases, not everyone in the addict's life will want him to quit. Those whose relationship with the addict took shape around the addiction (whether or not they are addicts themselves) might be frightened by the idea of such a fundamental change. "Will she still love me when she's sober?" is one of many scary and valid questions they may have.

If some friends and family don't share your sense of urgency about the problem, don't take it on yourself to persuade them. Trying to enlist reluctant people to your side can foster the addict's sense of persecution—and it can create more drama and debate for the addiction to feed on. With the support of those who share your concern, you'll become less concerned with negative influences and more confident as your family moves toward a healthier future.

Relearning Communication

Armed with all the guidance you've received in this chapter, it might be tempting to jump right in and start talking to your loved one about her addiction. But in real life, establishing a new way of communicating is trickier than it sounds in the pages of a book. Getting your communication habits into better shape takes practice and repetition.

Exercise 3: Communication Workout

This exercise gives you a safe way to start strengthening your new communication muscles by working them out.

1. Using a page in your journal, write a list of all the things you'd like to accomplish from a conversation with your loved one. Examples might include: "I'd like to clearly state how his addiction has affected me," "She learns that I'm done with our usual arguments," "He learns that I won't shield him from the consequences of his addiction anymore," and "She agrees to meet my sober friend." Maybe you'll write variations on all of those—and more.

2. When you're done with your list, pick out the goal that strikes you as the most important. Of course, you can't arrange the outcome of your conversation, and some of the desired results are entirely out of your control. But the process of deliberately choosing a single guiding purpose can help you to clarify your needs and priorities and to stay on track when emotions arise or your loved one tries to shift the conversation into a more familiar rut.

3. Keeping the goal in mind, write down some things you'd like to say to your loved one. For instance, if the goal is to tell your daughter that you won't let her in your house if she is using, you might write, "My door is always open to you, but I hate it when you're high. You constantly surprise us in the middle of the night screaming like a maniac to let you in. It scares me and your father—and the neighbors too. You look like a junkie. We're worried about you. But we won't open the door. We will call the police every time you are high and come here asking for money or a place to sleep. We love you, but we can't handle this anymore." Predict what your loved one might say in response, or rather, what the *addiction* might say, and how you would respond. Write it down.

4. Look at what you wrote in step 3. It's time to separate the helpful parts of your statements from the unhelpful ones. It's good to honestly report your emotional experience ("We're worried") but not to vent anger ("You look like a junkie"). Lightly cross out statements driven by emotions rather than observations, as well as those that seem like judgments, pleas, or demands. Are any of the statements about your loved one's behavior exaggerated or distorted? (The writer of the example in step 3 might ask herself whether her daughter is really "constantly" "screaming like a maniac" "in the middle of the night," or just occasionally speaking loudly in the late evening. And are the neighbors

really scared, or was that detail added for effect?) Cross out any such statements, along with threats (even, potentially, things like "We will call the police") that you're not sure you will carry out. Take your time.

5. Next, look at all the statements you crossed out. It's okay if a lot of them—or maybe all—are crossed out. Note that crossing them out doesn't mean that they're wrong or don't matter—just that they won't be effective in a conversation with your loved one. They might resemble some of the statements we discussed at the beginning of the chapter (statements that are pleading, demanding, blaming, and so on). Perhaps they speak to the symptoms of the addiction—or they reflect your emotional response to the symptoms—not to the addiction itself. Now take the time to rewrite the statements you crossed out. For instance, using the example above, "My door is always open to you" should be replaced with something like "I want to help, but only in ways that help you get sober." This step takes time and effort. You are redirecting your urge to use a communication style that has developed over the course of years or maybe decades. You can't expect to change overnight. Go easy on yourself. Rewrite as often as you need to. It might help to practice nightly, keeping your journal next to your bed.

6. Now you're ready to talk. Try to remember your helpful statements as you calmly talk to your loved one. When the conversation begins to veer off course—and it will—gently steer it back toward your goal (from step 2). Stick to the facts and keep judgments out. Even if the conversation is only thirty seconds long and ends with your loved one storming out, as long as you've stuck to the principles you've learned in this chapter, you can consider it a success. Congratulations.

7. Repeat steps 2 through 6 for the next goal on your list.

This approach can also steer you toward simple, unmistakable statements and away from soliloquies that will lose the addict's attention. Resist the temptation to try to address all of your goals in one conversation! Instead, try to stay focused on one goal. The remaining items on your list are there for future communications. Return to it whenever it feels appropriate, starting with the next-most-urgent goal.

Once you've established new communication habits with your loved one, it will be easier to have free-flowing conversations. But especially at first, it's helpful to stick to bite-sized messages.

What Now?

In this chapter, you've learned the best ways to get through to your loved one about his addiction. But I hope you've also learned that getting through to him isn't the main point of changing your communication habits. Giving voice to your own experience and opting out of pointless debates is, first and foremost, a way of getting through to *yourself*—of clarifying your own needs, desires, and priorities. You'll gain some peace of mind. You might even start developing stronger, healthier relationships in other facets of your life.

Breaking the silence is one of the first steps toward a new life. In the next chapter, we will tackle some of the toughest challenges of dealing with an addiction in the family. You'll learn how and why to set boundaries, how to protect yourself in dangerous situations, how to team up with others against the addiction, and more.

CHAPTER 4

Setting Strong Boundaries

My first boundaries were faint lines in the sand: "If he does this again, I won't..." When the lines were quickly crossed, I set stronger and more restrictive ones. But they didn't last, either. Sometimes, he just blew right past them. Other times, I bent them because it seemed like the right thing to do.

"I only need you to help me this one time," my brother would say, "and I'll never ask again." So I would help. The hard part of setting boundaries was the feeling that I was relinquishing control over helping him, because with each boundary, he became less and less a part of my life. It took years for me to learn how easily he could manipulate them.

As we saw in the previous chapter, habits and strategies that have served you well throughout your life may not be of much use when you're dealing with an addicted loved one. Simple, sensible premises like treating others the way you'd like to be treated and working together to find a compromise are easy targets for the manipulation addicts rely on to feed their addiction.

This chapter is your guide to the tough decisions that arise when one-on-one communication doesn't seem to work. Many people struggle to impose formal constraints on relationships with people they've known for years—or even their whole lives. Doing so can feel awkward, artificial, and just plain wrong. Your loved one may view such efforts as unwelcome intrusions into your relationship. He may say he feels hurt or betrayed that you didn't "just talk to him"—even if you've been trying for years to just talk to him.

These "intrusions" might involve activities such as clarifying what you will and won't do, denying requests for unhealthy kinds of help, and protecting yourself from potential violence. All of them are likely to come with some pain for everyone involved. But each of them, if done with care, can dramatically improve your situation and that of your family, in both practical and emotional terms. This chapter will help you decide when and how to take these actions.

Why Boundaries Are Important

At their best, boundaries can protect your well-being and help you avoid enabling behavior. Part of their appeal is that they seem so straightforward. In the chaos and confusion of addiction, straight lines are in short supply. But since boundaries are often at direct odds with behaviors, they often entail some painful feelings on both sides. Setting and maintaining them—and knowing when it's time to adjust them—takes some work.

Boundaries won't shield you from feeling sad or angry—or from the need to make difficult decisions. You won't suddenly become immune to the heartbreak of loving someone with an addiction. But in a situation in which so much is so confusing and vague and unreliable, a boundary can clear some space in your life that has been occupied by the addiction.

Family members of addicts are sometimes surprised to discover the extent to which they've neglected their own mental, emotional, and physical needs. Even people who've always had a healthy sense of boundaries can struggle to maintain them when an addiction enters their lives. For many people, it's the beginning of a new way of interacting with yourself—of taking the time to identify your own needs and treat them as seriously as you would the needs of a close friend.

Most feel like there's more they could be doing to help. As we've seen already, there's a whole lot you can do. But it's essential that you accept the limits of your power. When you take on another's recovery as your responsibility, you place yourself at the mercy of the addiction. From that position, it's very difficult to help yourself or the rest of your family. In effect, the addiction now has control over two family members instead of one.

The other main reason to set boundaries is strategic: addictions hate them. As we've learned, addictions feast on open-ended, flexible, negotiable situations, in which the addict can talk her way out of consequences, manipulate and confuse those around her, blame others, feel guilty about what she's done, and numb that guilt with more of the substance. By contrast, an addiction can't do much with a well-conceived boundary.

Here's how one sober alcoholic describes his experience with friends and family.

If someone didn't set clear boundaries, it was much easier to play them to get what I needed. Like if I asked to borrow money from my parents, even if they kind of knew I probably wouldn't pay them back, they would always fall back on their love for me and their fear about what would happen if I couldn't pay my rent. And after all, they could afford it. So there was always one more "just this last time." Until there wasn't. When I finally got cut off by my family, it was a wake-up call. It didn't get me sober, but that was kind of the beginning of [realizing] that what I was doing wasn't working anymore.

If your loved one has been given a boundary and has tested it and found that he can't move it, he'll know that one avenue toward getting what his addiction needs has been shut down. He may well find other resources, but he'll be less inclined to try to take advantage of the care his family feels for him. And somewhere inside, faintly, he may begin to hear the message that things have to change.

Boundaries vs. Deals

In some cases, a person might feel he's setting a boundary when he's really just negotiating a deal with the addiction. Issuing threats or offering rewards based on the addict's actions are classic examples. Such false boundaries are often much more comfortable to establish than true boundaries, because they don't really pose any danger to the addiction. As we've seen, negotiating with a disease doesn't work.

Threats and prizes might seem like opposites, but they're two forms of the same thing. They're both deals that are based on the delusion that you can control your loved one's behavior. (How could you, if she herself can't?)

If you've been dealing with an addict for a while, you've likely found yourself saying—or at least planning to say—"If you use, I'm never speaking to you again!" My first attempts to draw the line with my brother all sounded like that.

Here's why these conditional threats don't work:

- They're built around the addict's behavior. Whether or not the addict manages to fulfill his end of the bargain for a while, they encourage the delusion that the addict is in control.

- They're based on fear of future events, not on present reality. To an addict, this says that this boundary is up for adjustment, negotiation, and debate.

- They're hard to keep based on varying circumstances.

Promised rewards, such as "If you quit drinking, I'll help you with your car payments," are the mirror image of threats, but they work in exactly the same way. Again, rewards are built around the addict's behavior and based on future events that you have no control over. The promise of a substantial reward might be a reasonable way to motivate a nonaddict. But to an addiction, any promise that's incompatible with its one goal—

continued use of the substance—can serve only as an opportunity for manipulation. In the best-case scenario, the addict will stop—or *appear* to stop—just long enough to get the reward. He will get the car payment and then go back to drinking.

What a Strong Boundary Looks Like

So what do real boundaries look like? The best ones spring from a desire to protect yourself and to stop protecting the addiction. Unlike deals, they don't reward good behavior or punish bad behavior—arrangements that are easily manipulated. For example, the addict might think, *If I stay clean for a few days, he'll let me move back in* or *If it seems like I'm doing better, she'll start helping me with the rent again.*

Here are seven qualities every boundary should have:

- *It's sustainable.* Will you be willing to maintain your boundary even when your loved one complains that it's hurting her? Carefully consider this factor before establishing any boundary. For example, if your boundary is "I won't let you into the house if you've been using," will you be willing to uphold it if your loved one claims she has nowhere else to go?

- *It's clear.* The boundary should be simple, unmistakable, and nonnegotiable. For example, "I will help you pay for treatment, but I won't lend you money" is clear. "I can't bail you out of trouble anymore" is not.

- *It's about you, not the addict.* "I won't talk to you if I think you've been drinking" is a much stronger boundary than "I won't talk to you when you're drunk." That's because the former is based on your experience ("I *think* you've been drinking"), not on an arguable evaluation of your loved one's condition ("You're drunk").

- *It lightens your load.* Most strong boundaries cut off something the addiction wants, such as money, time, or protection from consequences. But remember, boundaries are about you. They should give you a feeling of relief, even when they're painful to keep.

- *It helps you in tough moments.* During a crisis, the impulse to help can be overpowering. A strong boundary can help you avoid reflexively saying yes to an urgent request for help that might not help the addict in the long run, such as an emergency loan.

- *It's in effect* now, *not at some point in the future.* A true boundary is neither a threat nor a promise. It is a report of your present reality.

- *You can change it later if* you *want to.* Boundaries don't have to be permanent to be effective. In fact, you should be able to adjust or remove a boundary when it no longer meets your needs or when you decide that immediate danger outweighs it. Boundaries won't insulate you from every tough decision. During an apparent emergency, you might have to quickly decide whether to take the addict's claims at face value.

If you do adjust or remove a boundary because of danger or because you can't bear the pain, that doesn't mean you're doomed to an unending cycle of manipulation. It means you're human. Never forget that a boundary is designed to serve your needs—and that those needs change over time.

When a Boundary Is Tested

In most cases, it won't take long before your boundaries are tested by your loved one either violating them or arguing against them. After all, the addiction needs to know what it's up against: does the boundary signal a real change in the relationship, or is it just more fodder for manipulation? It might take several tests before the boundary is confirmed as real and immovable.

Your loved one may claim to feel abandoned or betrayed by you. Tell him as calmly as possible that what you're doing is meant to protect yourself, not to punish him. It's fine to explain your reasons, such as "I'm scared of you when you're using" or "I think the money is feeding your addiction," as long as you keep the focus on your feelings and observations, rather than debating the specifics of the addict's behavior.

Communicating Your Boundaries

Since boundaries are all about you, they don't always have to be communicated to your loved one to be meaningful, but it can be very helpful to tell someone about them. Doing so can make it much easier to stick with a boundary in difficult moments—and to recognize when and why it's time to lift or adjust the restriction. (For more on that challenge, see exercise 5 later in this chapter.)

If you do tell your addicted loved one, keep in mind that presenting a strong boundary shouldn't be done angrily. The more calmly and simply you can communicate your boundaries, the less fear and guilt you give the addiction to work with.

An addict confronted with a new boundary will usually treat it as the opening statement of a debate. It's important not to engage, regardless of how reasonable (or ridiculous) her counterargument sounds. A boundary isn't a compromise. It's an existing reality that holds true no matter how your loved one responds to it. If you worry that a strongly negative reaction might cause you to shift the boundary, it may be wiser not to share it with your loved one, or at least not in person. If not telling her feels cruel, keep in mind that you are protecting yourself from the addiction, not punishing your loved one.

Dealing with Fear

Keeping a boundary can be scary. You might worry, for example, that if you stop supporting your loved one, he'll be forced to live on the street. Ask yourself how much of this expectation is based on a realistic assessment of the situation and how much is based on the illusion that you can control or protect him by keeping him near. Providing shelter might delay the worst consequences of his addiction, but it won't necessarily help him avoid them. At the same time, don't ignore or suppress your fear. Discussing this fear with a trusted person can help you to process the concern that could potentially make it difficult for you to maintain your boundary. A support group or therapist (see chapter 9) can also help you navigate this tricky territory.

Assessing Danger

Many family members of addicts eventually experience a boy-who-cried-wolf scenario. Years of drama and dishonesty make it difficult to know when someone is truly facing a life-threatening emergency (one that might lead you to consider bending your boundaries). Unfortunately, there's no magic formula for making the right decision. But there are a few key steps you can take when confronted with an apparent crisis:

- Get information from others. Relying solely on an addicted person's account of a situation greatly increases the risk of manipulation. If at all possible, get a second opinion about the threat from a nonaddicted source.

- Ask yourself if you're the right source of help. Are you truly the best-qualified person to address the situation—or only the easiest one for the addict to call upon? An addict will often claim that you're the *only* one who can help, but that's rarely the case. You're a family member, not the addict's lawyer or social worker or a paramedic (even if you happen to hold one of those jobs).

- Ask yourself whether continuing to shield your loved one from the full consequences of his addiction is more dangerous than the latest wolf at the door. Remember that substance addiction is, in itself, a life-threatening situation. Addicts put themselves at risk every day, and those who don't achieve sobriety face dismal long-term consequences.

If you feel guilty for even considering such factors in the midst of suffering, keep in mind that you didn't create this situation—the addiction did. Responding in the healthiest way for yourself, your family, and your addicted loved one might require you to make a decision that would seem coldhearted under normal circumstances.

When an Addict Asks for Help

If your loved one asks for help, that may be cause for celebration. But it's worth pausing to examine the request in more detail. Is she asking for help that will support treatment and recovery? Or is she requesting another kind of help, such as a loan or help covering her work or personal responsibilities? Providing any assistance aside from helping your loved one get treatment may only get you mired in enabling behaviors.

Be aware that your loved one may make the need sound like a short-term problem. She might say that she is waiting for a paycheck or a certain set of circumstances before she'll be able to enter treatment. It can take time to learn and accept the truth that delaying treatment will keep the addiction moving forward. Remember that addiction is a progressive disease. Its mental and physical grip on the addict is growing stronger even when she seems to be drinking or using less than usual.

How do you know when an addict genuinely wants the right kind of help? It's difficult.

Your instincts might not be of much use in these situations. Both hope (of how the help will improve things) and fear (of what will happen if you don't help) may be running so high that it can be hard to decide when to say yes. Keeping in mind that you're trying to protect both yourself and your loved one from the addiction, ask yourself five questions about any request for help:

- *How direct is it?* How many people or institutions stand between you and the care your loved one needs? For example, if your loved one asks you to pay for a stay in a rehab facility, and you pay the center directly, there's no way for your helpful actions to be manipulated. On the other hand, if you give your loved one cash or write a check in her name, there's no guarantee that money will reach the facility. The fewer steps between you and the end goal, the better.

- *How open-ended is it?* Vague requests such as a loan to "help me get back on my feet" or "buy some time" are the easiest for an addiction to exploit. Babysitting her children so she can have "a day to herself" might sound straightforward, but it could clear the way for her to use or get more of her substance. If you're not comfortable with the plans, gently saying no (and explaining why) might be the most loving thing you can do—even if doing it feels coldhearted.

- *How closely tied to recovery is it?* Lending your loved one your car is an open invitation to manipulation; giving him a ride to therapy or a 12-step meeting isn't.

- *Is it for someone else?* Be especially wary of help the addict is requesting on behalf of another party, including a child. What assurances do you have that the help will actually reach that person? If you decide to help that person, help directly, if possible.

- *Does it address the disease or just its symptoms?* When your loved one is in the grips of addiction, making the circumstances of his life a little easier won't get him to stop. Doing his grocery shopping so he can relax after a stressful day won't fix the problem.

Keep in mind that even if the help you're considering passes this test, you may well have other legitimate reasons to decline it, including your loved one's history, the results of help you have already provided, and your simply being unwilling to give more of your time, money, or energy. Stick to the boundaries you have set—or set new ones—when a request for help comes. Don't get into a debate about providing the help. An entirely sincere request might not always pass this test, and even if it does, you have every right to deny it.

Intervention

You've likely seen interventions in movies or reality television shows. These carefully planned events, in which family and friends confront an addict about the effect of her addiction on their lives, make for dramatic viewing. The addict either agrees to seek treatment or faces serious consequences, such as being cut off from communication or support. In effect, it's an aggressive form of setting boundaries.

Unfortunately, many viewers of these shows have attempted interventions without the planning, preparation, and expertise they require. The resulting confrontation can foster more confusion and anger rather than help to move both the addict and family toward recovery. I strongly recommend against staging an intervention without the guidance of a professional facilitator.

When to Consider an Intervention

Intervention should be considered only after attempts to speak to your loved one directly about his addiction, using the strategies described in this and the previous chapter, have failed to produce meaningful results. If that's the case, I recommend getting a feel for its goals, techniques, and dangers by reading more on the subject. The groundbreaking guide *Intervention*, by Vernon E. Johnson, and *Love First*, by Jeff and Debra Jay, can help you understand how the process fits into your family's long-term healing.

Professional Help

If intervention seems like a worthwhile option for your family, contact a professional intervention facilitator. As an outside expert unattached to your family, a facilitator stands the best chance of keeping an intervention from devolving into an emotional battle royal—an especially important advantage if your family's relationships are volatile. Before you hire a professional, make sure to meet with her in person and get a clear sense of her methods. The two books mentioned above can serve as a baseline for that conversation.

The Readiness Myth

Families sometimes delay asking an addicted loved one to get help, hoping the situation will improve on its own or believing that their loved one won't consider such an option until things have gotten much worse. In some cases, the family might even wait for a traumatic event or especially bad night, thinking it will make the addict more receptive to help. While that may be the case, waiting for such an event just invites more wreckage. Not every addict needs to hit a spectacular bottom before accepting help.

You don't have to figure out whether or not your loved one is ready for treatment. Addicts themselves often don't know until they try it. They might feel entirely ready but still hold on to a glimmer of hope that they can somehow moderate their substance use. Or they might *not* feel ready to quit but have reached such a point of desperation that they are willing to surrender and try anything. That point of desperation is different for every addict and won't necessarily correspond to a new low that's apparent to you or anyone else in your family.

A Word on Violence

Addicts can stray very far from their pre-addiction standards of behavior. That's true not only when they are under the influence of a substance but also when they're in desperate pursuit of it—or when something threatens their continued use. The boundaries described in this chapter can lead to outbursts of anger, especially when they establish serious obstacles for the addiction.

If any situation feels potentially volatile, err on the side of caution. If there is any history or signs of erratic or violent behavior, don't meet with your addicted loved one alone for potentially difficult conversations. If you ever fear for the safety of yourself or anyone else, don't hesitate to involve the police. Remember that you're doing it to protect yourself from the addiction, not to punish your loved one. Some recovering addicts describe their first brush with the law as an important wake-up call. For more about emotional and physical abuse, see chapter 7.

The chronic frustration of dealing with an addict can lead you to view it as an either-or situation, one in which you can help either your loved one or yourself. And at some point, you may have to make such a decision. But in the long run, the action that best protects your well-being usually turns out to be the most helpful for your loved one, even if it doesn't feel that way while it's happening. Taking care of yourself is an indispensable part of caring for your family.

The Right Boundaries

Boundaries work best when they're clearly tied to your priorities and goals. When you understand exactly what a particular boundary is *for*, you'll have an easier time sticking with it when it's tested. In this exercise, you'll learn to build boundaries based on what's most important to you.

Exercise 4: Building Boundaries

Start by listing three or four important goals or priorities related to your loved one's addiction, beginning with the phrase "It's important to me that..." Examples might include:

1. It's important to me that I not support his habit.

2. It's important to me that our kids are safe from their dad.

3. It's important to me that I stop running myself ragged trying to keep my niece out of trouble.

Next, create a boundary in keeping with each goal:

1. I won't give him money if he uses again.

2. If he comes home drunk, I won't allow him inside.

3. Starting next month, I won't help her out unless it's an emergency.

Finally, refer back to the list called "What a Strong Boundary Looks Like"—the seven qualities every boundary should have. One by one, compare each of your new boundaries against the list. Does it have all the hallmarks of an effective boundary? If not, adjust it until it does:

1. I won't give him money for anything. I will give money straight to a treatment center.

2. If I think he's drunk, I won't let him inside.

3. Starting now, I won't help her avoid trouble or bail her out of it.

As you work on your boundaries, one might emerge as the most—or even the only—important one to establish. Or you might find yourself coming up with more and more boundaries. If that's the case, don't hold back! Identifying your priorities and

translating them into sustainable rules gives you valuable practice identifying and protecting what's most important to you. Let
yourself rack up a long list; when you're done, you can figure out
which are the most important ones to establish. In either case,
congratulations! You've made a start toward establishing effective boundaries.

Adjusting Your Boundaries

It would be wonderful if you could just "set it and forget it"—
establish a carefully constructed boundary and walk away. After
all, aren't boundaries supposed to make things easier for you? But
like any effective fence, a strong boundary requires some mainte-
nance. If you want a boundary to truly serve you and your family,
you'll have to revisit it regularly, patch any broken sections, and
maybe eventually tear the thing down. This exercise will walk
you through that process.

Keep in mind that changing a boundary is not in itself a sign
of weakness, as long as it's you who are doing the changing and
you're changing it for healthy reasons. And figuring that out
takes some work.

Step 6 of the following exercise will help you double-check
your decision about adjusting a boundary. In relationships
untouched by addiction, we naturally want to help our loved
ones unless the help is bad for us. As we've seen, addiction com-
plicates that picture, in part because what the addict desperately
wants is often the worst possible thing for her. That's why it's
important to take a moment to put aside what your loved one
wants—and even what you want.

Exercise 5: Boundary Upkeep

Use your journal to periodically run your boundaries through the
steps below. They'll help you know when to make improvements
and when to leave things as they are.

1. Write the boundary in your journal. For example, "I won't interact with him in person except to get him to and from treatment."

2. What has prompted you to consider changing it? The answer might be that it no longer reflects current reality—such as if he's been sober and actively participating in recovery for a while. But it's important to be honest here and to go out of your way to consider motivations such as "I'm tired of feeling guilty for not talking to him," or, simply, "I miss him."

3. What are the risks of changing or removing the boundary? Would it leave you open to manipulation and deceit? What does the addict's history suggest might happen? Could loosening the boundary re-entangle you in your loved one's problems?

4. What are the rewards? Would restoring contact enable you to better support your loved one's recovery? Don't hesitate to list more selfish rewards, such as regaining closeness with someone you love. Such rewards are entirely valid; just don't use them to overlook potential risks.

5. If the risks outweigh the rewards or even give you pause, stop and consider keeping the boundary as it is—or even bolstering it to protect yourself from the present risks. If and when a change does seem reasonable, move on to step 6.

6. Use the technique you learned in exercise 2, "Be the Addiction." Put yourself in the addiction's shoes—and remember that an addiction doesn't end when the addict gets sober. Would the addiction be excited about the boundary change? If so, you should be extra cautious about any loosening. In some cases, simply communicating with your loved one—including a loving explanation of why you're keeping the boundary intact—can relieve the emotional discomfort that can cause people to remove boundaries prematurely.

Ultimately, only you can decide how and when to shift your boundaries. But exercise 5 can help you ensure that they're contributing to your ongoing recovery and growth rather than holding you back.

Intervention Letters

During the central activity of a typical intervention, friends and family members read letters to their addicted loved one about the effects the addiction has had on their own well-being and their relationship with her. Whether or not your family ultimately holds an intervention—and again, I don't recommend one without professional guidance—writing such a letter can help you better understand how the addiction has affected your life and can help you communicate that experience to others.

Exercise 6: Intervention Letter Rough Draft

Forget about spelling, grammar, and finding the perfect words. Just keep your pen moving. Your letter can be as long or as short as you need it to be. The following guidelines can help you stay on track, but don't let them slow you down. You can always revise your draft later.

Try to express love and concern, even when you also feel anger.

Address your loved one directly ("Dear Mom...").

Be specific about events and how you felt about them.

Cite examples of good times ("Remember when we used to go on walks?"), and how they've changed.

End with a request. What would you like the person to do?

When you're done, read what you've written. Does it surprise you? Many people affected by addicts don't recognize what they've been through until they see it on paper.

The intervention guidebooks I recommended above provide further guidance on writing these letters. But even if you never revise your letter or formally share it with anyone, writing and reading it can reinforce the validity and importance of your experience. Return to this exercise whenever you find yourself experiencing the "Is this really happening?" feeling that addiction so often creates.

What Now?

Everything we've learned so far has been oriented toward two goals: protecting your well-being and influencing your loved one toward accepting help. By now you might be wondering about the *kinds* of help I'm talking about and which one is best right now. Back in chapter 1, we learned that someone in the grip of an addiction is unlikely to stop—and stay stopped—on her own. Recovering addicts describe a wide range of journeys to sobriety, but almost all of them include plenty of help from others.

In the next three chapters, we'll examine the most common forms of treatment. You'll learn what to expect from each of these options and how they can help begin (or resume) your loved one's recovery journey. You'll also learn about the role you can play and how recovery can affect your family's relationships.

CHAPTER 5

Treatment Options

I lured my brother to the car using a bottle of whiskey. I was convinced that if I didn't get him to detox, he would die. As I drove—with him hunkered down in the backseat with his bottle—it became blazingly apparent to me that I was more interested in his survival than he was. It wouldn't be the last time that thought would cross my mind. My brother had already stayed at a long-term-care therapeutic community for a year and a half and then relapsed within a few days of discharge.

At my parents' house, this very docile man became violent. When my mother refused to buy him a bottle of vodka, he threatened to slit her throat in her sleep. Terrified, my parents reluctantly called the police and got a restraining order. When he returned and tried to break in the front door, he was taken to jail.

I received a call from my brother to pick him up from jail. As a condition of me coming to get him, he agreed to go back to rehab the following day. I put him in a hotel that night, afraid to bring him home with me. In the morning, when I went to get him to treatment, he was already gone.

The term *treatment* represents a range of organized programs and services designed to help addicts achieve sobriety. This chapter will help you explore and understand your loved one's treatment options, starting with safe detoxification. You'll learn what to expect from several different kinds of treatment, the best questions to ask when evaluating a program, and how you can help your loved one get the most out of the care she chooses.

But before we begin, you might be wondering why treatment is important in the first place—and whether it's really worth the disruption and expense. We've all heard stories of celebrities entering rehab, only to relapse a month or a year later. Isn't that evidence that treatment doesn't work? The short answer is *yes*. On its own, without follow-up, support, and ongoing effort, treatment won't keep your loved one sober. In that sense, treatment doesn't "work." It won't fix your loved one or cure his addiction. My brother's story is just further proof of that.

So why bother? Because the right program can help your loved one lay down a strong foundation for a lifetime of sobriety. Without such a foundation, he'll have a much harder time staying sober—or returning to recovery if he does relapse. By addressing the psychological, physical, and emotional problems underlying his addiction, treatment gives your loved one a better chance at long-term sobriety.

Detoxification: Just the Beginning

The first step in the treatment of addiction is weaning the body off the addictive substance. This process, known as *detoxification* or *detox*, is the essential first step in any treatment, and it is the step most feared by addicts, because of its physical and emotional discomfort. The prospect of your loved one's detox can be scary for you, too. Gaining a general sense of what to expect can take some of the fear and uncertainty out of the situation.

The detox process begins with an addict who is either intoxicated or has recently stopped using a substance. When she has been without the substance for a period of time, she begins to feel the physical symptoms of withdrawal. These symptoms vary by substance and user, but some of the most common are anxiety, irritability, insomnia, sweating, heart palpitations, nausea, and digestive problems. Ideally, the addict stays at a detox facility until the symptoms reach a safe or tolerable level. Medications are sometimes provided to ease the symptoms, and the addict is observed around the clock.

Withdrawal Dangers

Alcohol detoxification involves more than discomfort. The risk of seizure or a medical condition called *delirium tremens* makes withdrawing from alcohol dangerous, especially for all-day, everyday drinkers.

Not to be confused with "the shakes"—the anxiety and shakiness that typify most alcohol withdrawal—delirium tremens (or "the DTs") is a potentially life-threatening condition. Symptoms usually begin after up to seventy-two hours of abstinence and can include severe anxiety and confusion, diarrhea, insomnia, fever, rapid heart rate, and high blood pressure. The withdrawing alcoholic may experience intense perceptual disturbances and visual, auditory, or tactile hallucinations. Alcoholics who have previously experienced a seizure or the DTs are at high risk; it's critical that they not attempt withdrawal without medical supervision.

Withdrawal from benzodiazepines (tranquilizers) can also be dangerous. Among long-term users, severe and life-threatening withdrawal symptoms such as seizures can result from a rapid reduction in usage. (Note that even gradual reduction entails some seizure risk.) These symptoms may sometimes appear days after stopping the substance, when an addict thinks he is out of danger. Barbiturate withdrawal can produce similar difficulties.

While withdrawal from opiates is less dangerous in itself, it still carries serious risks, especially if other health conditions are present. Whether you're aware of such complications or not, it's safest to seek out a residential detox facility. These organizations may also arrange for the continuation of care, transferring your loved one into an inpatient facility or partial hospital program.

Detox Medications

Medications can be used to alleviate some of the intense symptoms of detox. These drugs can be given in a detox facility or, in some circumstances, can be prescribed by a doctor and taken home to complete the detoxification process. In the case of patients completing detoxification at home, it is important that medications are taken exactly as prescribed and, if at all possible, monitored by a family member or loved one. As with most medication, the effect will not necessarily be increased by taking more than the prescribed dosage. If symptoms or concerns persist, call the prescribing physician.

Methadone has long been used as a form of opioid replacement therapy. It acts on the same brain receptors as heroin and morphine but is both less pleasurable and less debilitating. In some limited cases, it can enable a nonfunctioning addict to begin functioning again. Treatment professionals disagree about the effectiveness of replacement therapy. In my opinion, methadone use too often becomes another limiting addiction, rather than a step toward recovery. Methadone is obtained from a program or clinic that dispenses the medication on a daily basis. Patients must go to the location until the point when they are able to bring limited amounts home or be weaned off the drug. Methadone can, however, be a viable option when other avenues have been eliminated and when chronic relapse has warranted another type of intervention.

With the introduction of Suboxone, a branded name for buprenorphine and naloxone, which is also used for opiate detoxification, certified physicians can send addicts home with a prescription (unlike with methadone). If used under strict supervision for a very limited time, Suboxone can be a highly effective and safe detoxification protocol. The drug eliminates withdrawal and partially blocks opioid effects, but some addicts will not use the drug correctly, instead turning it into a way to maintain their high.

All of the medications used in detox have a place and a particular use that can be successful. While efforts to reduce the pain of withdrawal are important, clinically, I don't believe withdrawal that is totally free of discomfort is ideal, since it completely shields the addict from some of the real consequences of addiction. The emotional and physical pain of withdrawal is an experience the addict will not wish to repeat.

Hospital or Home?

Unless an addict is at risk for the withdrawal dangers described above or has a medical condition that is exacerbated by physical stress to the body, most detoxes *can* be done at home. That doesn't mean they *should*. Home detox can invite a host of other problems, medical and otherwise. If your loved one has an unknown medical condition or has lied or omitted information about his history, home-based detox can be especially risky.

Detoxing can be a difficult and frightening experience not just for the addict but also for anyone who witnesses it. While you might have a strong instinct to take care of your loved one, "hosting" a detox can be a heavy emotional burden to take on, especially if he becomes demonstrative or combative. Another concern is that at home, he might likely have easier access to his drug of choice than he would in a clinical setting. During a period of physical and emotional discomfort—which the substance would instantly relieve—this situation can invite relapse. Furthermore, detox medications can also be abused. For these reasons, whenever possible, professional assistance and monitoring away from the home environment is the best choice.

A third option for detoxification, called *ambulatory detox*, may prove to be more economical and convenient than a hospital-based scenario. This is a partial hospital program or an intensive outpatient program that can appropriately monitor the detox process while the addict is still living at home. You should know, however, that some insurance companies may not recognize this level of treatment. And it's important to note that the state rules for providing treatment may restrict or prohibit this service in some states.

How Long Does Detox Take?

Total detoxification varies from person to person and substance to substance. Acute withdrawal (or the worst part of it) generally occurs during the first few days or up to a week. By the end of the second week, addicts usually begin to feel relatively well physically. If prolonged substance abuse has injured the body or brain, withdrawal can be longer and more intense. In some cases of benzodiazepine addiction, withdrawal may take months.

Most addicts experience intermittent symptoms long after the first two weeks, such as depression, anxiety, irritability, mood swings, and cravings. These symptoms—sometimes grouped under the term *post-acute withdrawal syndrome*—may come and go over the course of the first year or two of sobriety. Because these discouraging symptoms can contribute to relapse, they highlight the need for ongoing treatment. It can be helpful to encourage your loved one to think of the symptoms as growing pains, a temporary condition experienced as her body and mind adjust to life without her substance.

Choosing the Right Kind of Treatment

Of course, detoxifying the body does not eliminate the addiction. Further treatment is imperative for long-term recovery. I have found that the longer an addict stays in a sober and therapeutic environment, the greater the likelihood of long-term recovery. When rehab treatment can be maintained for a couple of months, deeper issues can be addressed.

Unfortunately, most addicts start with shorter, less-intensive treatment. As a general but reliable rule, addicts need more help than they think. Don't be surprised if your loved one insists that all he needs is a few days of detox. Pride, financial constraints, or denial may keep your loved one from committing to the level of care needed. The idea of setting aside one's normal life—even if that life has become miserable—can be a scary and humiliating prospect.

While you can't force someone to enter a particular form of treatment (assuming he's over eighteen), you can support him in getting the most effective help possible. Most likely, he isn't in any condition to learn about the options available to him; by taking on that work, you can steer him toward a thorough, effective program.

If your loved one doesn't choose the form of treatment you think he needs, don't get caught up in arguing about it. Take encouragement from the fact that your loved one is accepting help for his addiction.

Mental Health Evaluation and Treatment

It's natural to want to believe that all that is needed is to stay away from addictive substances. But addiction is a medical condition with lasting psychological and behavioral ramifications. For most addicts, stopping—and staying stopped—requires some deeper work. Often the psychological dependence on the substance is where the hard work of relapse prevention comes in. As you evaluate programs, look for one with a strong mental health component.

Successful mental health treatment begins with a thorough evaluation of the client, including pre-addiction history. Observations from family members can also be helpful. The most useful diagnostic tool, however, is seeing addicts in a structured environment where abstinence from the substance is certain. This allows professionals to observe an addict when the fog of the substance begins to lift.

Note that a psychiatric evaluation upon admission to treatment is unlikely to predict who needs medication and who does not. The behaviors of active addicts mimic those of many mental illnesses, and those symptoms may disappear with abstinence. On the other hand, if an underlying mental illness exists, it will flourish when self-medication stops.

Inpatient Treatment: What to Expect

You've likely seen representations of inpatient, or residential, pro-grams on television and in movies. Addicts check into and stay in a hospital-like (or, in some cases, resort-like) facility for the duration of their care. Whether leaving your loved one at such a facility feels like a great relief, a scary challenge, or some combi-nation of the two, learning the basics of these programs will help you rest easier while he's away—and will help you support his continuing recovery when he comes home.

The typical length of stay is about a month, although insur-ance companies rarely provide full thirty-day coverage, and there is no evidence to support the effectiveness of that specific dura-tion. Research *has* shown, however, that lengthier stays produce better outcomes (Simpson, Joe, and Brown 1997; National Institute on Drug Abuse 2002; National Institute on Drug Abuse 2012).

Some addicts come to a treatment center agreeing to stay a certain length of time. The length of this period might be dic-tated by the courts or negotiated with family members, or it may be based on the addict's own assessment of how long he can or should stay. Once detox symptoms have eased, therapy is under way, and the addict is in better condition to make decisions, this agreement can be revisited.

Treatment in an inpatient facility may include group therapy, individual therapy, psychiatry, medication management, dis-charge planning, and introduction to 12-step programs. Additional activities beyond traditional clinical protocols, such as exercise, yoga, and meditation, can also enhance treatment. Many higher-end facilities also provide services such as massage therapy and acupuncture.

Intake

Although the admission and treatment process is relatively standard for most facilities, every treatment center has details unique to its culture and state regulations. Unless mandated by a court, or the patient is under eighteen, drug and alcohol treatment is voluntary. Participants are required to sign themselves in and are free to sign themselves out.

Upon arrival, the patient's current situation is evaluated for safety factors, such as level of intoxication and risk of seizure. In most states, American Society of Addiction Medicine (ASAM) criteria must be met to justify admission to a treatment program. These criteria are based on medical, physical, and psychological factors; you can learn the basics at http://www.asam.org. If ASAM criteria for inpatient treatment are not met, a referral is made to the appropriate level of care, such as a detoxification program or an intensive outpatient program. If admission *is* warranted, an individual treatment plan is designed. This personalized plan maps out the care, identifies the problems that need to be addressed, and proposes how goals will be achieved.

For safety, possessions—and sometimes the individual—are searched, and a drug test is administered. This is followed by getting settled in his room and oriented to the program schedule. Treatment usually starts the same day.

The Treatment Team

Your loved one's treatment team may include a primary therapist, who handles her case; group therapists, who conduct day-to-day treatment; a utilization review manager, who maintains insurance authorizations and financial arrangements; a psychiatrist or nurse practitioner, who assesses and maintains medication needs; and administrators.

A psychiatric evaluation takes place within a day or so of admission. Group counseling also starts shortly after admission (or after your loved one completes the detox process, if she hasn't already). Drug counselors monitor and guide the groups, incorporating education, problem-solving skills, and behavioral modification tools. Individual counseling focuses more closely on the client's particular issues.

Many treatment centers base the nonclinical part of their services on supportive programs such as Alcoholics Anonymous. During treatment, residents might be expected to read 12-step books, attend meetings (sometimes with members of the AA community who are not residents), and even begin "working the steps." Other facilities offer alternative support systems such as SMART recovery. SMART recovery (self management and recovery training) is a secular, scientifically based recovery program that focuses on four concepts of building motivation, coping with urges, problem solving, and lifestyle balance.

A Typical Month

Everyone's experience in rehab is different, but having watched thousands of addicts go through treatment, I've noticed some unmistakable patterns. Since you likely won't have close contact with your loved one throughout her stay—more on that later—it can be reassuring to have a sense of what she might be experiencing. Here's a week-by-week account of a typical month-long stay in an inpatient facility:

WEEK 1

The days right after detoxification move slowly. Your loved one will have meetings with her counselor and treatment team, but she may not absorb all the information she receives. She begins to make friends with other residents. (Strong bonds can form quickly among addicts, who have all faced many of the same struggles.) She might struggle with insomnia, appetite loss, depression, and the side effects of any medication she's taking to ease withdrawal or to begin treating mental health issues. But toward the end of the week, she might start to experience glimmers of hope about the possibility of a new life.

WEEK 2

Now that the discomfort of withdrawal has mostly passed, she may feel energized (though sleep may still be an issue). Addicts commonly mistake physical improvement for having a handle on their addiction; many of them begin focusing on their discharge date. Your loved one may want to leave treatment, thinking that she "gets it" now and doesn't need further help. Don't be surprised if she calls, asking you to come pick her up. At this point, therapy changes gears and attempts to slow her down, helping her realize that her psychological addiction remains in full force.

Family members may be invited to participate in a session. Family sessions can shine a light on how her addictive behaviors affected her loved ones. This is a very important step in the recovery process, and one I encourage you to participate in.

WEEK 3

By this point, it has probably become clear to the treatment team whether she's actively working toward her recovery or is just biding her time until she's released. Deeper, more challenging psychological issues, such as grief, often emerge and must be confronted. These might spring from such losses as a death or from the more intangible losses caused by the addiction—including her dreams and her sense of self. Other therapies, such as anger management, may also begin to show results. The discharge planning team reevaluates her needs and considers a potential discharge date based on the progress being made.

WEEK 4

She's making steady progress. Lost weight is regained, medication is kicking in, and the appearance of health is clear. She may develop a false sense of security. Remember that only a month ago, this person was totally out of touch with reality.

Discharge is planned and discussed with the addict and all interested parties, including insurers and family. Insurance coverage usually dictates what treatment should continue and what should end. Sometimes this sends a person home thinking that she has everything under control, while the clinical team knows that much more work is still ahead. Sometimes an agreement is reached that more time is required for healing. Goals are reassessed, and the team evaluates how much longer is needed.

Contacting and Visiting Your Loved One

Most inpatient programs limit contact with the outside world to a few phone calls a week or a single visitation day. The desire to connect can be strong on both ends, but except for participation in a family-oriented program at the facility, there really is no need for close contact with home. Addicts should be focusing on themselves during treatment—and realistically, they're in no condition to provide support, remedy a problem, or affect anything that may be going on in the outside world. Remember that even though your loved one is no longer under the influence of substances, she is still heavily influenced by her addiction. Don't be surprised if she looks for any excuse to leave treatment. That's true *especially* if the program seems effective—that is, if it presents a real threat to the addiction. Your loved one might suddenly decide, for example, that she simply has to get back to her responsibilities at home or work—even if she's been unable to meet those responsibilities for years! Or she might claim an unresolvable conflict with another resident or a staff member. By limiting contact to light conversation and words of encouragement, you make it easier for her to stay in treatment.

Discharge Planning

The transition from rehab back to normal life can be jarring for everyone. Thorough discharge planning by the facility's staff helps ensure all parties are as prepared as possible for reentry. This planning should address where the recovering person is going and what treatment, if any, he needs when he graduates from the current program. The treatment team is more likely to recommend discharge when the addict is displaying stable behavior, is showing a positive response to any prescribed medications, and has demonstrated the ability to use newly learned tools to respond to the triggers he'll encounter at home and work.

In some cases, the discharge team makes a clinical suggestion that the addict relocate in order to separate herself from environmental influences or abusive relationships. This is particularly common if an addict has made repeated attempts at recovery and has returned to the same situation again and again. In such cases, the discharge team should help find appropriate housing and follow-up services. If the addict is at all hesitant about discharge, the discharge team should encourage her to stay and address the reason for her uncertainty or, at minimum, to identify what's troubling her. Unfortunately, insurers often determine that these issues can be handled on an outpatient basis. When an addict can't afford to continue his stay, the facility has no option but to discharge an addict to a lower level of care. A therapist at the facility should help him process his uncertainty, and he should be provided with contacts or referrals before discharge.

Outpatient Treatment: What to Expect

For many families, the appeal of outpatient programs is obvious. They can give you a sense of hope without requiring you to be apart from your loved one—or to cover her responsibilities while she's away.

Outpatient treatment typically consists of individual or group counseling (or both) provided by licensed mental health counselors. Individual counseling typically consists of one hour-long session per week; group counseling sessions usually last an hour or two and take place once or twice a week.

Intensive outpatient programs (IOPs) are typically run three hours a day for three or more days per week, though some offer treatment seven days a week. Clients live at home during this treatment. IOP programs address basic topics that affect recovery, with the goal of helping addicts return to normal lives. They are commonly attended by addicts who are making their first attempt to get clean and may not be willing or able to undergo more intensive treatment. IOPs may also serve as a continuation of care for those being discharged from another program.

In addition to the three-hour group sessions, IOP participants typically receive one hour of individual counseling a week. Some facilities also provide psychiatric care, if needed. Failure at the IOP level—meaning the inability to stay clean or sober— results in referral to a higher level of care, such as an inpatient residential treatment or a partial hospital program (including detox, if needed).

Since it's cheaper and less disruptive than inpatient treatment, an IOP is an attractive option for many addicts and families. But it's also easier to stray from than an inpatient program, in which all aspects of the addict's experience are geared toward recovery. It can provide the illusion that progress is being made without truly undermining the addiction. That said, if the addict is committed to staying clean and sober, IOP treatment can be effective. In my experience, it's best used as continuing care after a higher level of treatment is completed.

Partial Hospital or Partial Care: What to Expect

Partial hospital programs (PHPs) or partial care (PC) programs are better known in the mental health field as *day programs*. A PHP/PC offers a more flexible and independent living arrangement than an inpatient facility but otherwise provides similar services. The cost is consequently lower. Your loved one attends a full day of treatment programs in outpatient facilities, then returns home at night. Services are rendered four to six hours a day, five to seven days a week.

Clients in a PHP/PC typically get more hours of therapy than in inpatient facilities, but fewer institutional services, such as daily or around-the-clock medical services, nursing, physical therapy, and holistic medical services. The same options for psychiatric care are offered; medical care is provided, though to a lesser extent; and the environment is less restrictive than in an inpatient facility. Many PHP/PC programs offer sober housing for clients while attending treatment—"day and night" programs. The housing arrangements in day and night programs can vary greatly, from beautiful homes to motel rooms. Day and night programs resemble an inpatient program in that the client stays in contact with the treatment facility around the clock and lives in a structured, sober environment. But since there is minimal supervision and no overnight nursing staff, they are not a good fit for people who need close monitoring for medical issues.

Some states do not allow day and night programs, but in those states, many PHP/PC programs offer an alternative in which the treatment schedule is coordinated with an independent sober living environment (SLE, which I'll discuss in the next chapter). The housing services are not included in the cost of treatment, however.

Therapeutic Communities: What to Expect

Therapeutic communities (TCs) are structured, drug-free environments where people live together, usually with a therapist, to change their behaviors and learn new coping methods. TCs take a holistic approach to recovery, not just treating symptoms, but also working toward the addict's reintegration into the "real" world, including long-term employment and healthy personal relationships. Most participants stay in these communities for more than a year. Unsurprisingly, those who stay in treatment longer have better outcomes than those who leave early (Vanderplasschen et al. 2013).

TCs can be mandated—for instance, as a condition of release from prison—or can be sought out independently by people who need ongoing behavior modification. TCs are usually funded by charity services and government aid, along with fees paid by the addict; insurance rarely covers this type of treatment.

A review of sixteen studies found that TCs appeared to generate significantly better outcomes than other recovery options (Vanderplasschen et al. 2013). TCs also seem to work best for addicts who need a lot of community support to rebuild their lives (De Leon 2010; Brunette, Mueser, and Drake 2004).

Health Insurance and the Cost of Treatment

The cost of treatment can be one of the most important issues to investigate as you research help for the addict in your life. It can also be a source of added stress during an already difficult time— especially if you try to tackle it alone. If possible, ask a family member or friend to share the challenge with you.

Treatment can be expensive, but keep in mind that it's almost always much cheaper than an ongoing addiction. (When you add medical and legal expenses, lost employment, and miscellaneous wreckage to the direct cost of drugs and alcohol, the total can quickly become staggering.) What follows is a brief overview of current conditions; please note that they're always changing.

Understanding Your Loved One's Coverage

Start by talking to your loved one's insurance provider to make sure you understand the policy's benefits, limits, and deductibles. Use that information, along with the fees charged by the center, to create a ballpark estimate of your loved one's potential out-of-pocket expenses. (Note that most inpatient facilities currently cost between $10,000 and $30,000 per month; high-end facilities may charge much more.) A good treatment center may also be able to provide guidance about coverage for its services. Many facilities will get the needed insurance authorizations and approvals for you, but it's your responsibility to understand what is and is not covered.

If coverage has been denied, the insurance company should send you an explanation of the reason for denial and your options for further review or appeal. If the facility is handling the insurance, they will most likely also handle the appeals. Note that you can have a dramatic impact on this process. Keep in touch with both the facility and the insurance representatives handling your claims, and ask whether there are any calls you can make to improve the situation. If you think coverage was wrongly denied, and the appeal options provided by the insurance company don't yield results, first speak to a supervisor at the insurance company and then contact your state insurance commissioner's office.

A Bit of Background

Since 2008, US insurance companies have been required by law to offer coverage for mental illness and substance-use disorders at the same level as, and with no more limitations than, medical and surgical coverage. But in response to this "parity" law, insurance companies began covering only the parts of such treatment justified by medical necessity. This strategy has enabled them to restrict access and limit the length of covered treatment.

Covered length of stay has been reduced, even for facilities within the insurance company's network. What insurance covers is not always the same as what professionals have found to be effective. Reimbursements often don't even meet the provider's expenses for services required by state regulations.

Coverage by Type of Treatment

Insurance companies monitor services to control their costs. Outpatient treatment, also known as individual counseling, is the least expensive type of treatment, followed by IOP, PHP/PC, inpatient, and finally detoxification. Here's a basic breakdown of coverage by treatment type, as of this writing:

- *Detoxification.* Insurers will cover detoxification if the addict is experiencing symptoms that warrant medical care. Once acute symptoms have subsided, it is not likely that continued detox treatment will be authorized. The average length of stay in a detox is three to five days, with some lasting as long as two weeks, in cases involving complications or benzodiazepines.

- *Inpatient treatment.* Most policies provide an average of two weeks of inpatient care, barely enough time for patients to get through withdrawal, adjust, and begin to understand the new concepts of recovery. After detox, inpatient care is sometimes not authorized at all, depending upon the history of previous treatment and severity of use and withdrawal. Some policies do cover longer inpatient stays, however, so be sure to check your loved one's policy.

- *Partial hospital programs or partial care.* PHP/PC services typically cost about half of what inpatient services cost, but at present, most insurance policies will not cover this level of care without proof of medical necessity. Many policies won't cover PHP/PCs that provide housing, or they will cover the treatment, but not the housing component. Insurance requires PHP/PC participants to be independent and seeking employment, living at home, or residing in a sober living environment.

- *Intensive outpatient programs.* Insurance companies have also reduced authorization for IOP services, which continue to have many participants. Even with these reductions and the limits on the number of covered treatment days per week, outpatient programs are the most widely covered option as of this writing.

If you're struggling with the cost of treatment, note that community-oriented treatment centers run by nonprofit organizations may provide much less expensive (or even free) treatment in your area. These options have given many addicts and alcoholics a start toward long-term sobriety. Call 211 for information about resources where you live.

Space is often limited in all of these programs; be sure to put your loved one's name on the waiting list of any program that might help him. (These lists often move quickly.) In many areas, the Salvation Army and other religiously based programs have residential substance-abuse units that provide free—and in some cases readily available—services. Residents are required to work or contribute to community services while receiving treatment.

Although 12-step fellowships such as Alcoholics Anonymous and Narcotics Anonymous are not treatment, they are free and available in most communities. They provide a supportive environment and many resources that may help you and your loved one find further care.

Ten Key Questions to Ask

Whether your loved one is considering detoxification, inpatient, outpatient, or PHP treatment, the quality of programs varies widely. Unfortunately, online reviews tend to be biased—both positively and negatively—according to the reviewer's personal experiences, rather than assessing the quality of care she received. Statistics about a program's effectiveness, if available, tend to be vague or unreliable. (How long does someone have to remain sober to count as a success? How does the program know who relapses?) These limitations make it all the more important to vet the program yourself. Here are ten key questions to ask.

- Is the staff adequately trained? (And what does the facility consider adequate?) Are there licensed therapists on staff? Do treatment providers hold advanced college degrees, or only training certifications? Those with certifications may be quite competent, but a staff that also includes degrees in various disciplines is ideal.

- What does the treatment consist of? To what extent, if any, is it based on 12-step programs? If there is a well-founded bias for or against these groups, this is an important factor to consider. For more about 12-step programs, see the next chapter.

- Is psychiatric care (treatment for mental illness) provided? If so, how is follow-up for the psychiatric care completed?

- How much access will your loved one have to her counselors? Do clients see their therapist once a week or only once during treatment? States have different requirements for individual counseling during different levels of care. Does the facility simply meet minimum requirements for treatment, or does it exceed them?

- How personalized is the care? I'm not talking about the legally required "individualized treatment plan." Truly personalized care means that when specific needs are discovered, the facility is versatile enough to thoroughly address them.

- How will the family be involved? Are observations from family members used in treatment? Does the program direct the family to resources for their own ongoing support?

- When you call, with whom are you speaking? Are you able to reach a live person? Most reputable addiction treatment facilities have a receptionist or admission coordinator skilled in providing basic information.

- Who runs or owns the facility, and for how long have they done so? How are they involved in the care? Are they therapists? What are their credentials? Feel free to ask to speak to the owner, administrator, clinical director, or a therapist. Reputable programs should have no problem putting you in contact with them. (Note, however, that their time may be limited.)

- Does the program have a clear set of rules governing participant behavior? Effective programs have well-defined rules. What's the policy on smoking? For inpatient facilities, what is your loved one allowed to bring? What kind of food is served, and when? Is there a "blackout" period after arrival—a few days to a week of no outside communication, designed to reduce the risk of early departure? For residents who are parents, what's the policy on contact with their children?

- How does the program handle discharge? What kind of follow-up care is offered? If your loved one requires extended treatment, can the facility keep him for as long as needed, provided that financial arrangements have been made?

Beware of hard-sell tactics and aggressive marketing. If answers seem less than transparent, or if you can't reach someone in charge, look elsewhere. Don't feel pressure to accept a facility you're not comfortable with. Note that many 800-number helplines that appear to be government-run are actually using clever marketing tools designed to funnel you toward a specific facility. If you begin to feel confused, breathe for a moment and then ask for help from a friend or family member who may have fresh input.

Treatment and the Criminal Justice System

In some cases, you or your loved one might not have much say in his treatment options. A treatment program is often mandated by a judge for drug- or alcohol-related offenses. It can be

presented as an alternative to jail or prison time, or as a condition of probation.

Most jails and prisons have treatment programs, and many
are regularly visited by members of 12-step programs. Nevertheless,
only about one out of every nine US inmates who suffer from
substance abuse or addiction receives any treatment during his or
her incarceration (National Center on Addiction and Substance
Abuse 2010). This is due to limited space in programs, varying
degrees of willingness on the part of addicts, and other factors.

Your Power and Its Limits

For many family members of addicts, the prospect of treatment
provides a welcome opportunity to help without fear of enabling
the addiction. Helping your loved one choose and enter a good
treatment program can be very gratifying. But in the wake of this
victory, it can be easy to slip into believing that the problem has
been solved or that you can control more than you actually can.
As your family heads into this stage of recovery, it's important to
remind yourself of both your power and its limits. This quick list
can help.

Some things are within your control:

- helping to find and choose a treatment option

- helping him pay for treatment (*if* you want to and can
  afford it)

- avoiding contact that distracts him from his treatment

- participating in family treatment sessions

- taking care of yourself

Some things are outside your control:

- whether your loved one enters treatment

- whether he chooses the treatment you'd prefer

- whether he stays in treatment

- whether he takes treatment seriously

- whether he stays sober after treatment

This lack of control doesn't mean you shouldn't be hopeful. By even considering treatment, your loved one has taken critical steps to admit to himself and others that he can't solve the problem on his own. That is a very encouraging sign. If you're able to provide meaningful help, while also recognizing and accepting the limits of that help, that's cause for celebration.

When Your Loved One Is in Treatment

You won't magically stop worrying just because your loved one is in treatment. But you can take advantage of her time away to return your focus to the things *you* need. Take this time to heal, relax, and renew your energy. Are there activities you used to enjoy that have fallen by the wayside during your loved one's struggles? A class you've wanted to take or a trip you've been meaning to plan? Relationships that have been neglected or damaged?

Exercise 7: Recharge

This exercise is designed to help you get back in touch with what sustains you.

1. Close your eyes and think of yourself at a happy time. What are you doing in that moment? Open your eyes and write down a quick description of the activity. Don't worry if it's not what you think you "should" be doing. Repeat this process until you've written down ten feel-good activities.

2. Review your list and cross out any activities that don't leave you feeling happy *after* doing them or that have negative consequences. There's no need to label these activities as bad or unhealthy; they're simply ones that don't feed your well-being.

3. For each of the remaining activities, ask yourself when you'll realistically be able to do it next. Your answer might be "tonight," if the activity is cooking a nice meal for yourself, or "next year," if it's traveling the world.

4. Take steps *right now* to do the earliest available activity on your list. Even if that action is to pull out your phone to make an appointment for a later date, be proud of yourself for taking a step right now.

5. Plan to do the others when your schedule allows. Write down potential future dates so that you have a goal to work toward and time frame to work within. Make a commitment to yourself not to go longer than a couple of days without doing something kind for yourself.

What Now?

In this chapter, you've learned how to help your loved one find effective treatment. I hope you've also learned that even if she enters a reputable rehab facility, receives excellent professional treatment, forges strong bonds with other recovering addicts, and comes home determined to put her newfound coping skills to work, she won't be cured of her addiction. In the next chapter, we'll take a look at the important period after treatment. You'll learn about follow-up and ongoing treatment, sober living environments, and ways to support your loved one's promising new direction without her falling back into old habits.

CHAPTER 6

Supporting Your Loved One's Recovery

After he left treatment, Chris went to his girlfriend's house to continue his recovery. I quickly coordinated the lab tests and other procedures necessary for him to get a new medication that would make it impossible for him to get drunk. To qualify for his first injection, he had to stay sober for ten days. We talked daily, and he went to his meetings. When a very long week and a half had passed, and it was finally time for his appointment, my old fear came back, just as strong as ever. I wondered if he'd really show up. And he did! He then continued to do so on a monthly basis for over a year. I couldn't do it for him, but I did help him get the catalyst that ultimately changed the course of his life.

The day treatment is completed can be a joyous one. You finally have your brother or wife or nephew or daughter back, without the substance abuse and all the damage and drama that went with it. It's tempting to view this moment as the end of the addiction phase of your loved one's—and your family's—life. However, take caution with this notion. There's still a long road ahead, and while it's heartening to see a straight and smooth path stretch out before you, the reality is that bumps and turns are part of the journey.

It's much wiser to think of the homecoming as the beginning of the recovery stage. Regardless of how effective your loved one's treatment has been, she didn't come home cured of her addiction. To stay sober after initial treatment, almost all addicts require ongoing help—likely for the rest of their lives.

Remember that the gravitational pull of the addiction is still in effect. Without taking daily action in the opposite direction—the continuous efforts collectively called *recovery*—she will likely slip back into drinking or using. Sadly, relapse in the days and weeks after treatment is common. However, the longer an addict stays sober, the less chance of relapse. One study of 1,162 addicts found that roughly two-thirds of those who were sober for less than a year relapsed in the following year. After a year, fewer than half relapsed during the following year, and after five years, fewer than 15 percent did (Dennis, Foss, and Scott 2007). Fortunately, there's plenty you can do to help your loved one achieve long-term sobriety.

Welcoming Your Loved One Home

Many family members expect that when their loved one returns home, life will return to the way it was during happier times, before the addiction took hold. While it's true that newfound sobriety is a wonderful development, it's important to recognize that it won't make everything perfect.

Expect the Unexpected

Living without their substance is a fundamental shift for addicts. You might be surprised by how different your loved one seems. And as thrilled as you are about his sobriety, you might not love *all* the changes in his behavior. Newly sober addicts can be moody, irritable, and raw. All the feelings the substance has suppressed may suddenly come to the surface, and your loved one is still learning to deal with them and express them. And some addicts may be so "into" what they've learned in treatment that they even seem a bit sanctimonious—suddenly they've got all the answers.

It can be useful to think of someone in early recovery, regardless of his age, as an adolescent. Don't take all the awkwardness as a sign that recovery isn't working or that he is doomed to return to using. Shifts in mood or personality traits might simply signal that he's struggling to deal with life on its own terms. The duration of this adjustment period will vary from person to person.

The Case for Patience

In addition to caring deeply, you and other family members might have built up a backlog of negative feelings. The anger and frustration you've felt for years won't evaporate just because the destructive behavior has stopped. When your loved one doesn't seem as apologetic or grateful as you'd like—or doesn't seem to grasp what his addiction has done to the family—it can be tempting to confront him. You might want to say all the things he wasn't willing or able to hear when he was drinking or using. You have every right to do that.

But my experience working with families of addicts has shown me that patience in early recovery usually pays off—assuming that the addict is actively working toward recovery. As we'll see in the next chapter, family relationships take time to heal. The recovering person will be much better equipped to participate in that process when he's on firmer ground. For now, the most powerful thing you can do is support his recovery efforts.

How to Help in Early Recovery

Now that the substance use has stopped, skillful support can have more impact than ever. Keep in mind that the decision to

help is yours; some family members choose to minimize interaction until their loved one has stayed sober for a long period. If
you choose to help—whether right away or in a few months—
here's how to do it wisely.

Five Key Dos

Many of the tools you've gained in previous chapters can be
applied to early sobriety, but this delicate period also comes with
some special considerations.

DO ACKNOWLEDGE WHAT YOUR
LOVED ONE IS DOING

For many addicts, staying sober for the first few months will
be the hardest thing they've ever done. Just making it through an
hour—let alone a day—without using or drinking can feel like a
colossal challenge. Let him know you appreciate the difficulty of
what he's doing. If you're not an addict, don't pretend to know
how your loved one feels. Instead, you might say something like,
"I can only imagine how hard this is."

DO ENCOURAGE ACTION

Isolation and inactivity are ideal conditions for an addiction
looking to worm its way back. Staying busy won't fix an addiction, but it can help your loved one avoid falling into the obsessive negative thinking that can lead to relapse. Try to steer
conversations with her toward what she's *doing*, not just how she's
feeling. For example, you might ask "What are you up to today?"
rather than "How are you doing?"

Similarly, note that the addicts who "talk the talk" the
loudest—the ones who say all the right things about their
amazing progress in a 12-step or other recovery program—aren't
always the ones who are truly committed to recovery. Perfect-
sounding messages can be a smokescreen for the addiction. If she

says she's "doing great," follow up with specific questions: What has changed for her? What can she tell you about the program she's in? By showing that you're genuinely interested in her experience—and don't just want to hear the magic words that will let you stop worrying—you make it more likely that she'll open up if she's in danger of relapse.

DO HELP HIM PUT RECOVERY FIRST

Most addicts leaving treatment are greeted by a range of pressures: making up for missed work, finding a new job, repaying debts, resuming childcare. Making it to every therapy session or aftercare appointment or 12-step meeting can seem trivial by comparison.

One of the best ways to help is to make it easier for your loved one to take part in recovery activities. That might mean driving him to a meeting or appointment. To ease your burden, collaborate with other family members and friends whenever possible.

Providing this help can feel frustrating or even infuriating. Your loved one is finally sober—isn't it about time he started pulling his weight? This point of view is totally justified, but it's not the most effective one. That's because his ability to meet *any* responsibility depends on his recovery. By making it easier for him to put recovery first, you can improve his chances of avoiding relapse.

DO HAVE FUN

Early recovery is a period of abrupt change for everyone your loved one's life touches. During what can be a tense time, a purposeless afternoon at the park or at the movies can help everyone breathe easier. Addicts sometimes need help remembering how to blow off steam without their substance. Suggest an activity he used to enjoy—one that might take his mind off his troubles.

And keep in mind that letting yourself laugh, whether he's laughing along or not, is one of the best things you can do for yourself. You deserve a break!

DO PAY ATTENTION

It's normal for a person to feel anxious or moody after quitting a substance she's relied on for years (see the description of post-acute withdrawal syndrome in chapter 5, in the section "How Long Does Detox Take?"). But keep an eye out for erratic behavior or extreme lethargy or hyperactivity, which might signal a mental health problem that requires professional help. If you observe such signs, talk to her about your concerns and don't hesitate to contact her doctor or treatment facility—ideally with your loved one's participation.

Also be aware of the warning signs of relapse. These can include a return to behavior associated with substance abuse, such as spending time with old drug and drinking buddies, lying, statements of hopelessness about recovery, and a general "who cares" attitude. If you think he might be about to relapse, tell him why you're concerned and offer to help him get in touch with his recovery resources—such as his therapist or 12-step peers—right away. For more guidance about relapse, see the exercise at the end of this chapter.

Five Key Don'ts

Early recovery can be a time of great hope and relief for you and your family. But it's no time to ease up on the loving but cautious approach you've been developing. Here are some of the most common mistakes to avoid.

DON'T SWEAT THE SMALL STUFF

Early sobriety isn't the time to focus on relatively minor problems such as annoying personal habits or unresolved disagreements. Quitting cigarettes, for example, can wait. This doesn't mean you should give him a free pass, but by giving him a little leeway on other matters for now, you might help him focus on the recovery that will improve his ability to handle problems of all sizes down the road.

DON'T TAKE OVER

Ultimately, recovery from addiction requires the addict to take action. You can play a powerful supporting role, but you can't force someone to recover. The path to recovery you have in mind might not be the one she needs. Micromanaging your loved one's schedule or assuming a parental role (if you're not her parent) can impede her progress toward personal responsibility.

DON'T CODDLE

It's natural to want to be soothing during a scary period like early sobriety. That's a caring impulse, but overdoing it can encourage passivity. Remember that your loved one has gone to great lengths to avoid harsh realities for years. Even if she doesn't return to her substance, this habit of escape can be a hard one to break. Don't feed into it by babying her. The most loving thing you can do is to encourage positive action: meeting with other addicts in recovery, receiving therapy or other ongoing treatment, and getting physical exercise. If she isn't willing to participate in her recovery, your assurances won't do her any good.

DON'T LET YOUR GUARD DOWN

The addiction may be dormant, but it's still on the lookout for opportunities to get your loved one back to drinking or using. You can be loving and supportive while maintaining the discerning eye for manipulation you developed reading the previous chapters. Don't stop being selective about the kinds of help you provide. Review the section "When an Addict Asks for Help" in chapter 4.

When you recognize dishonest or manipulative behavior, be open and honest about it. You might say, for example, "Hearing you say that, I'm worried that you might be setting yourself up to use again." If you fear angering your loved one with such a statement, remember that your silence is exactly what the addiction wants.

Most addicts fresh out of treatment are bombarded with conflicting internal messages. In one ear, they hear all the stuff they learned about addiction in treatment. In the other, they hear the familiar voice of the addiction, saying, "One drink won't hurt" or "You're better now—you can handle it." This voice is at its most convincing when your loved one confuses it for her own (Trimpey 1996). By calling attention to manipulative behavior, you can help reduce its power.

DON'T OVERLOOK YOUR OWN NEEDS

After years of worrying, it can be gratifying to support a positive new direction. That can make it tempting to put your loved one's recovery at the center of your life. If you do that, your well-being is still at the mercy of your someone else's behavior, just like it was when she was drinking or using.

How can you help both of you become more independent at the same time? We'll delve into that subject in the chapters ahead. For now, ask yourself if you're *choosing* to help. If you feel motivated by a sense of obligation or guilt rather than personal choice, it might be time to take a step back from the relationship.

What to Do About Triggers

For an addict, a trigger is anything that spurs an intense desire for a substance. Seeing (or smelling or even hearing) the substance itself is the most obvious trigger. But neighborhoods, people, and situations associated with drinking or using can be just as powerful.

In treatment, some of his triggers should have been identified and a plan created for avoiding them. Talk with him about potential triggers and how you can help. But keep in mind that he might not be aware of all his triggers, especially if this is his first attempt at sobriety. If the recovering person lives with you, keep all addictive substances—not just his favorite one—out of the house.

When there is not easy access to a substance, a momentary crisis or lapse in judgment has a better chance of blowing over. When that happens, your loved one gains another day of sobriety—and the chance for the addiction's grip to loosen a little bit more. For addicts in active recovery, triggers lose their power over time.

Ongoing Treatment and Support

Just about every reputable treatment center teaches addicts that recovering from addiction is an ongoing process. Your loved one's chances of long-term sobriety improve greatly if she's willing to actively participate in that process. Understanding the different kinds of help available to her can help you support her recovery.

The Role of Therapy

It's estimated that between one-third and one-half of all drug and alcohol abusers also have a mental illness or mental health condition (National Alliance on Mental Illness n. d.). For some, underlying psychological problems don't come to light until sobriety, because the substance abuse had been suppressing or distorting the symptoms.

For successful long-term sobriety, an integrative therapeutic approach—one that can address the addiction *and* the mental illness—is essential. This can be a long-term project, extending well beyond rehab. Weekly or biweekly psychotherapy sessions can help. Psychotherapy is a process of counseling that can be done in several environments: individually with a licensed therapist, in a group environment in a rehabilitation facility, or a combination of both. If your loved one found one therapist particularly helpful in inpatient or outpatient treatment, sessions with that therapist can sometimes be continued. If she hasn't found therapy useful so far, a new therapist may provide a fresh perspective and a sense of progress in recovery.

Many recovering addicts who *don't* suffer from acute mental health issues can also benefit greatly from professional help, especially in the early months and years of sobriety. In some cases, psychological challenges related to abuse, relationships, family dysfunction, physical health, and other concerns must be addressed in order for recovery to take root. Even Alcoholics Anonymous, which emphasizes a spiritual solution to addiction, says, "we should never belittle a good doctor or psychiatrist. Their services are often indispensable in treating a newcomer and in following his case afterward" (2001, 133).

Almost all therapists are familiar with addiction, but most don't make it their primary focus. Some addicts require an addiction specialist; others are best served by one with more general training in both addiction and mental health. Such concerns shouldn't stop your loved one from making a first appointment. Finding the right therapist is partly a matter of personal rapport and comfort, and it may require some trial and error. The important thing is to start looking.

While in therapy, there will be emotional and psychological changes. These changes might include subtle, unconscious shifts as well as deliberate behavioral changes. A therapist won't tell your loved one what to do; ultimately, she will adopt the information and ideas that suit her. As with everything else associated with addiction, the benefits of therapy aren't likely to occur on a schedule. Changes are sometimes dramatic, but they're more often gradual. In some cases, seeds are planted that don't bear fruit until long after therapy has ended. Note that information about a participant in therapy is confidential and can be revealed only with the client's permission. Treatment is a highly sensitive and personal issue. The therapy team cannot tell you anything about the therapy without a signed release of information from the client. As much as you may want to help or be aware of the progress, it is not an area that can be negotiated, due to confidentiality laws.

12-Step Programs

In part because they're free, 12-step programs are by far the most popular type of recovery program. The original 12-step program, Alcoholics Anonymous, was founded in the 1930s by alcoholics who were trying to find a way to stay sober. The core of the program is a set of 12 actions, ranging from admitting that they couldn't control their drinking (step 1) to helping other alcoholics achieve sobriety (step 12). Taking these actions—or "working the steps"—is AA's suggested method of achieving freedom from alcoholism. For the complete text of AA's 12 steps, see the appendix.

Groups that focus on other addictions, such as Narcotics Anonymous, have slightly adapted AA's 12 steps, but the key principles are the same.

WHAT ARE THEY ALL ABOUT?

You've likely heard a wide range of opinions about 12-step programs. Even members of those groups differ about what makes them work. The "party line" you'll hear most often at 12-step meetings is that working the steps with the help of a sponsor—someone who participated in the fellowship for a more than a year with continued sobriety and who is willing to guide a new member through the steps—is the key to continued sobriety.

But some members say the sense of community with other recovering addicts is what matters most. And more spiritually inclined members may emphasize a personal "spiritual awakening" brought about by the steps. Still others cite a combination of all those factors.

MEETINGS

Most 12-step meetings take place weekly and last about an hour. At some point during the meeting, a basket is passed; members who can afford to do so are encouraged to make a small donation (typically a dollar or two) to cover expenses.

Beyond those similarities, meetings are all over the map. Some consist of a handful of people chatting around a table; others pack auditoriums. Some are based on reading and commenting on 12-step books; others on sharing personal experiences. One addict's warm and welcoming gathering might seem like noisy chaos to another. If your loved one disliked his first meeting, you might encourage him to "shop around." Many areas have groups specifically for young people, as well as men-only and women-only meetings. You're free to attend any meeting marked "open" ("closed" meetings are for addicts only).

REPLACING OLD RELATIONSHIPS

For newly sober addicts, the friendships formed by socializing before and after a 12-step meeting can be just as important as the content of the meeting itself. To stay sober, distance is needed from the friends they drank or did drugs with. If those friends are clean and sober, caution is still needed in reentering these relationships due to common history, and thus reentering them is not recommended. Replacing those relationships with new ones built around recovery is one of the most powerful changes that can take place in early recovery.

DO THE PROGRAMS WORK?

Contradictory reports about 12-step success rates are easy to find; reliable statistics are not. Definitions and methods seem to vary with just about every study. For example, how long a period of continuous sobriety defines *success*? At what point in time is sobriety measured? What defines a *member* of a 12-step program? Nevertheless, according to a 2009 survey of available reports,

"Multiple studies evaluating the efficacy of AA both as a stand-alone treatment and in comparison to other treatment models point to the substantial and ever-increasing body of literature that suggests that regular posttreatment attendance in 12-step programs significantly improves alcohol and other drug use outcomes" (Straussner and Byrne 2009).

One thing about 12-step programs that seems beyond debate is that they *don't* work well for addicts who aren't willing to put in the effort they require. Those who expect a 12-step program to work the same way a drink or a drug does—automatically and instantaneously—will be disappointed. "It works if you work it" is a common refrain at meetings; this work usually includes creating a thorough personal inventory, acknowledging and making amends for past wrongs, and helping other addicts. A personal inventory is a fearless and honest look at who you are and the flaws you have. This includes the impact these behaviors and flaws have had on others.

GOD AND THE 12 STEPS

The 12 steps are expressly designed to bring about a "spiritual awakening." Many addicts are wary of this part of the program and the presence of the word *God* in the 12 steps. Though many meeting spaces are rented from religious organizations, AA is not affiliated with any organized religion.

The steps themselves encourage members to develop their own understanding of and connection to a power greater than themselves. For any number of addicts at a meeting, there might be an equal number of different conceptions of this "higher power." For some, it's the God of their religious upbringing; for others, it's their "true self"; others rely on nature or the universe or an indefinable sense of something bigger than they are. Some agnostic and atheist members even see *God* as an acronym for "Good Orderly Direction." In my opinion, some addicts use their reservations about religion as an excuse to reject 12-step programs, when the real issue is the commitment and work these programs require.

Other Recovery Programs

If you don't live in a big city, it can feel like 12-step programs are the only game in town. That's not necessarily the case. Some addicts who have ties to a particular religious tradition are greatly helped by becoming more involved in them. At the secular end of the spectrum, several organizations offer recovery programs based on rational or psychological principles rather than spiritual ones. These include SMART Recovery, Women for Sobriety, LifeRing Secular Recovery, and Secular Organizations for Sobriety (SOS). None of these options are nearly as widespread as 12-step programs; search the web for options where you live, as well as for groups that meet online.

Sober Living Environments

Some addicts need extra help making the transition from treatment back to the stresses of normal life. A sober living environment (SLE) is a home shared by recovering addicts and alcoholics. Some SLEs are privately run and based in private homes; others are affiliated with treatment programs in a dorm or apartment-style environment. Residents pay rent, follow house rules, and share household chores. They're usually required to attend 12-step meetings and submit to drug tests (and they are kicked out if they drink or use drugs). Typically, a longtime resident serves as house manager but does not provide formal counseling of any sort. Rather, he or she is there to enforce the house rules and ensure safety of the residents.

An SLE can be ideal for an addict who needs structure and thrives on close fellowship with others in recovery. Addicts who "need their space" will have a harder time, but even they can benefit from a stay in an SLE, especially if they've had difficulty staying sober in a less structured environment. The quality of SLEs varies greatly. Look for one that's been in operation for years and has credible online reviews. Before signing a lease, your loved one should be sure to visit the home, meet the house manager, and understand all the house rules.

Two Roads

I've provided a lot of advice in this chapter about supporting recovery. Because there's so much you can do—and because you care so much—it can be easy to cross over into assuming responsibility for your loved one's recovery. Now is a good time to remind yourself that her recovery is not your own.

Your support in early sobriety can be a gift she cherishes for the rest of her life. But just as nothing you do can make her drink or use, nothing you do can keep her sober. No matter what happens or what your interaction is, it is solely the decision of the addict to use or drink. Recognizing and accepting this reality is a giant stride down the path of your own recovery.

One way to do this is to plan what to do in the event she relapses. At first glance, planning for relapse might seem like a pessimistic, untrusting activity. Aren't you supposed to be helping to create a positive, supportive environment for recovery? Think about it this way: no one wants or expects to face a fire, but just about everyone knows exactly what to do in the event of one. There are a number of ways a plan is helpful:

- The sad truth is that most addicts who achieve long-term sobriety didn't succeed on their first try: 40 to 60 percent of addicts relapse within a year of their discharge from treatment (McLellan et al. 2000). If your loved one does relapse, a plan will give you a better chance of quickly offering effective support, not just an emotional reaction. This can help make the difference between a brief slip and a return to full-time active addiction.

- It provides peace of mind for you and other family members. No one wants a relapse to happen, but having a response plan in place can make the prospect less fearsome.

- It helps foster a family culture of openly addressing real possibilities—the opposite of the silent denial that addiction thrives on.

Exercise 8: Create a Relapse Response Plan

Start a new page in your journal and answer the questions below, one by one. Before each answer, write the heading for that question (for example, "1. Safety"). Take your time; some of the questions will require you to do a little research or talk to friends and family members.

These questions require you to imagine some tough circumstances. If you start to feel overwhelmed, put this exercise aside and come back to it later.

1. **Safety:** Remind yourself here to call 911 in any emergency. It might sound obvious, but the intense feelings a relapse can bring can cloud your judgment. If you're afraid of—or for—your loved one when he's drinking or using, or if he refuses to leave your home, are you willing to contact the police?

2. **Recovery contact:** If your loved one is involved in a 12-step program, is she willing to give you the name and number of her sponsor or another friend in recovery? Helping fellow addicts who've relapsed is a key part of those programs. Especially if your loved one feels ashamed about relapsing, she may be more receptive to help from her fellow addicts, most of whom have been through relapse themselves.

3. **Outside support:** Which family members or friends can help? Ask others now if they'd be willing to provide transportation, childcare, or companionship so you're not alone with the addict, or other forms of help, as appropriate. Sharing the burden can greatly ease the stress relapse can bring.

4. **Detox:** What detoxification options are available locally? These can include hospitals, treatment centers, and dedicated detox facilities. Include phone numbers.

5. **Treatment:** Will you encourage your loved one to enter a treatment program after detox? If so, will you suggest escalating from his most recent treatment to the next level (from outpatient to inpatient, for example)? What kind of treatment are you willing to help pay for, if any? Research local options online and list their names and phone numbers.

6. **Housing:** If the addict lives with you, will you allow him to continue doing so after a relapse, either during or after treatment? If not, search online for local sober living environments and list them here.

7. **Boundaries:** Revisit the section "What a Strong Boundary Looks Like" in chapter 4 and exercise 4. Would a relapse require you to add a new boundary or adjust your existing boundaries? If so, how? If your loved one refuses help, how will you respond?

Congratulations on finishing a tough job. Please take a moment to remind yourself that you may never need to use this list. I'm sure filling it out was difficult, but I hope you'll find over time that it takes some of the fear out of the possibility of relapse. Revisit your plan regularly, updating it as relationships change and as you learn more about treatment options.

Now What?

In the first half of this book, you've learned a lot about your loved one and how you can help him. The rest of this book is more interested in *you*. (Don't worry, your loved one will make plenty of appearances—after all, he's an important person in your life.) In the next chapter, I'll show you how you can begin healing relationships that have been damaged or limited by addiction.

CHAPTER 7

Healing Family Relationships

One night I got a phone call from the state police. A tollbooth operator had reported that my brother had been driving erratically on the expressway. His car was impounded, and he was taken to the state psychiatric hospital for evaluation. Once again, he had relapsed, this time causing a condition called drug-induced psychosis, in which he thought he was being followed.

He came home to my parents' house, returned to treatment, and then moved into a sober living house. Again he rebuilt his life, this time getting a good job and moving up the ladder there quickly. His life was seemingly good. He was taking medication, had met a woman, and had decided to remarry.

The marriage lasted only two years and ended the same as his first marriage had: due to relapse. Eventually, he also lost his job. He was now forty-six years old. His son was grown now and had never known him. Everything he had worked so hard for in his sober years was going away. His disease accelerated, and he began smoking crack cocaine and drinking. Homeless once again, he stayed in drug-infested motels.

My mother, now elderly, was no longer able to handle the stress. My father had died, and I was now the owner of

*a drug-treatment facility. My mother and I agreed once
again to let him go.*

*So we planned his funeral and prepared ourselves for the
approaching reality. It was our way of separating the man
we knew from the addict he had become—and our way of
facing the severity of the situation.*

The effects of an addiction on the rest of the family aren't always
as dramatic as they were on mine. Family members themselves
often don't realize the degree to which the addiction has affected
their thinking, their behavior, and their relationships. But that
can make it even harder to know how to begin healing, even if
the addict has stopped drinking or using.

This chapter will help you understand how addiction has
affected your family relationships, including those with children
and your spouse or partner. Then I'll show you what you can do
to help all those relationships not only recuperate from the effects
of the addiction but also start growing in healthier, more satisfying directions.

How Addiction Affects the Family

An addiction usually dominates the relationship you have with
the addict. But it can also affect a whole family's network of bonds
and responsibilities. That might sound grim, but the effect isn't
always completely negative. In some cases, the shared experience
of dealing with an addiction brings a family closer together, ultimately making it stronger than ever. That, however, usually doesn't
happen without plenty of work. And before that work takes place,
it's helpful to understand what has already happened.

The Domino Effect

A common way that addiction spreads its influence is by ini-
tiating a chain reaction in family relationships. Take the example

of an addicted father and husband. Because he's unreliable, his wife has to take over almost all of the parenting duties. The most obvious impact is that the children get one frazzled parent instead of two effective ones. But it also means she has less time to spend with her sister, for whom she's always been an important source of emotional support. The sister then has a harder time at work and with her other relationships. And so on—the effects keep rippling outward.

Unfortunately, once the substance abuse is removed from the equation, all those supporting relationships don't just snap back into place. That doesn't mean the changes are irreversible; it only means that things won't simply return to the way they were before the addiction took hold. To truly recover, a family has to develop new ways of interacting with one another.

Breaking the Orbit

Families with an addicted member often develop a centralized structure, in which everyone's well-being revolves around the addict. Whether or not the addiction is openly discussed, it seems to preoccupy most family members. When the addict is sober, everything's okay—for the moment. When she goes off the rails, everyone is terrified. In both cases, the addict is the center of attention and the heart of the family's emotional life. That's a no-win situation: the fear of a relapse can be almost as stressful as dealing with an active addiction.

The healthiest, most resilient families aren't dependent on the behavior of one person, but are instead made up of multiple strong bonds among different family members. In such a family, no one is overly dependent on any other. Instead, the family is made up of many different relationships based on mutual support and shared responsibility. When one family member is addicted or preoccupied by another's addiction, it doesn't topple the rest of the family. If your go-to sister disconnects, you still have your cousin or uncle or mother-in-law.

Different People, Different Responses

An addiction in the family puts pressure on all of its members. Faced with such a scary and frustrating situation, people react in a wide variety of ways. One family member might want to cut ties with the addict, while another might insist on keeping the addict safe, no matter what. Meanwhile, a third member might deny that there's a serious problem at all. Gender differences sometimes play a role in these responses: women are more likely to nurture or help; men, to confront or withdraw. There's also a lack of widely shared knowledge in our culture about effective ways to deal with addiction.

Because the stakes are so high, these strategic disagreements can deepen into long-lasting interpersonal conflicts, some of which may remain in place long after the addict himself has entered recovery and regained control over his life. Family members may also develop resentments about who's shouldering how much of the load. It's common for several people in a family to feel like they're the ones pulling all the weight. The good news is that there's plenty you can do to counter these divisive effects.

Help the Healing Begin

Helping your family grow in a healthier direction isn't easy, especially if the addict is the head of the family or if the family has been obsessed for years with the addict's condition. But over time, it can happen. Here are nine good ways to get started.

- *Talk.* As we've seen, addiction does some of its worst damage in silence and secrecy, which allow shame, guilt, and misunderstanding to thrive. In some families damaged by addiction, each member suffers in isolation. Openly discussing what's going on can greatly ease the emotional strain for everyone, but especially for children.

- *Broaden the discussion.* When every family conversation seems to circle back to the addict, it reinforces the idea that the family's well-being depends on him. This is true—and equally unhealthy—whether the addict's most recent behavior is terrifying or encouraging. Make a point of bringing up topics that have been neglected while the family has been preoccupied by the addiction. For example, at the dinner table, make sure to ask about and acknowledge what's going on with other family members.

- *Reconnect.* Are there family members you've drifted away from since the onset of the addiction? In addition to love and support, these people can provide different perspectives on the experience—an especially helpful benefit if you and your closest family members have been stuck in old habits while responding to your addicted loved one.

- *Respect differences.* No two family members will respond to the pain of addiction in the same way. Your uncle may pull back from the family rather than wanting to bond. Your sister may repeatedly vent about the addict's past behavior instead of talking about what's going on now. It's important to let others respond in their own ways. Remember that your relationship with the addict is different from everyone else's.

- *Know your role.* When the addict and the people hit hardest by the addiction are outside of your inner family circle, proceed with extra caution. Inserting yourself into conflicts you may not fully understand won't help anyone heal. Play a supporting role without taking sides. That means offering empathy and maybe some practical help, as well as encouraging and supporting any family member's recovery efforts (for example, taking your cousin to an Al-Anon meeting). When tempted to provide advice, share your own experience instead.

- *Don't lecture.* In response to the loneliness of loving an addict, it can feel especially important to get other family members to see things your way. Keep in mind that you're all in this together—not because you all see things the same way, but because you're a family and you've shared a painful experience. When discussing the addiction, frame it in terms of your own experience rather than pointing out what others should be noticing, experiencing, or doing.

- *Reinforce basics.* You might all differ in *how* you respond to addiction, but you've all experienced some pain. Simple expressions of love and concern—even a sincere "How are you?" or "I know this has been hard for you"—can go a long way.

- *Focus on the here and now.* The pain of dealing with an addiction can increase everyone's tendency to reminisce about the good old days or to speculate about brighter days ahead. Both of these pastimes can give you temporary comfort, but they won't help your family heal. When your mind is on the past or future, you can't be fully engaged with the people who are right in front of you. And without that engagement, your relationships won't grow stronger.

- *Question guilt and blame.* It's heartbreakingly common for a family member to think that if she—or another family member—had just acted differently or said the right thing at the right time, the addiction wouldn't have taken hold. As you've learned, addiction doesn't work that way. If a family member is suffering from this kind of misconception, you can help by sharing what you know (without forcing your views on him). It can be very powerful to have habitual feelings of guilt or blame questioned by a loving family member.

All of these actions can help, but none is as important as patience. Some family members may need to keep their distance until they feel safe enough to come back into the fold—perhaps after the addict has remained sober for a prolonged period. Remember, too, that every member of the family is dealing with her own struggles and challenges in addition to what the addiction has brought. Give the healing process time.

Family Therapy

Just about any family dealing with an addiction can benefit from family therapy, in which the therapist addresses the whole family system and all the interactions within it. Each member has her own personal experience of addiction; helping each person understand the others' positions and struggles can greatly decrease conflict and misunderstandings.

Family therapy usually begins while the addict is in treatment. This stage of therapy might be minimal—one or two sessions with a therapist at the treatment center or a group session with other families present—but it can be extremely helpful. These early sessions often focus on enlightening your loved one about how his disease has affected the family. It's often the first chance family members have to honestly share their feelings about the addiction in a safe and supportive environment.

Speaking your mind and heart in such a setting isn't just freeing for you and other family members. For your addicted loved one, recognizing the damage the addiction has done is an essential step toward recovery. Although addicts tend to be aware on some level that their behavior has had an impact, they've usually minimized and justified it in order to keep using. Family therapy can bring the true impact to light and shift the focus from the individual to the family.

The addict doesn't have to be present for family therapy to have a powerful impact. As we've seen, an addiction can damage and distort relationships throughout the family. Therapy can help a family address and repair those effects, in part by helping family members develop more open and effective communication.

Children and Addiction

Sadly, addiction often hits children the hardest, especially if the addict is their parent. When an adult who is supposed to protect and guide a child doesn't meet those responsibilities—and sometimes doesn't even seem like the same person from one moment to the next—that child will begin to feel deeply unsafe. Even if the household isn't violent or chaotic, children are often scared of *and* for their addicted parent. In such a fearful atmosphere, the play and exploration that typify a healthy childhood are often impossible.

The effects of addiction aren't always obvious from a child's behavior, but the damage can be deep and lasting. Children of addicts often develop low self-esteem, and many wonder if the addiction is their fault (Dayton 2006). They're also more likely to develop addictions themselves and to suffer from emotional, psychological, and social problems for the rest of their lives (National Association for Children of Alcoholics n. d.). (I'll discuss how to help addicted young people in the next chapter.)

Talking to Children About Addiction

While living with an addict is a tremendous burden for children to carry, it can be overcome. Love and support from the stable individuals in their lives can help them navigate the scary, confusing experience they're facing.

Talking to kids about addiction in a helpful, age-appropriate way is tricky. Start by recognizing what you won't be able to fully explain. Most children won't be able to grasp why Daddy keeps making himself sick—after all, he usually doesn't understand it himself. But kids of all ages do understand what being sick means. In fact, because they have fewer preconceptions, children often have an easier time viewing addiction as a disease than many adults do.

Addiction is a complicated topic. When talking to children about an addict in the family, it's best to keep things simple. The US Substance Abuse and Mental Health Services Administration (SAMHSA) offers three core suggestions (McCoy, 2009):

- *Encourage children to express their feelings.* Children who are dealing with drug abuse in their families can benefit from talking about how they feel. They may have issues with trust, so guide them toward reliable adults who care for and want to help support them.

- *Emphasize that addiction is an illness.* It's important for children to understand that an addiction to alcohol or drugs is an illness that can be treated. Tell them what type of therapies will be used, and explain how the treatment can help the family member recover.

- *Tell children they aren't to blame.* Sometimes children think that a problem in the house is their fault. Let children know that they are not to blame for the addiction and that there is nothing they could have done to prevent it.

To these fundamental guidelines, I'd add one more: that it can be very helpful, when talking to children, to acknowledge the sadness and scariness of the situation for you and other family members. Many parents think they have to put on a happy face for their kids, but doing so may only intensify the cognitive dissonance the child has likely experienced—the difference between what adults say and the scary, uncertain way things actually seem. Showing children that their fear and sadness are normal reactions can take some of the overwhelming power out of those emotions.

Be sure to also take advantage of the resources available from school, such as a counselor or school psychologist, and organizations devoted to children of addicts and alcoholics. The National Association for Children of Alcoholics is one such organization.

Its "Seven Cs" is a teaching tool designed to help children begin to understand addiction. The Cs are embedded in the following statement: "I didn't **cause** it. I can't **cure** it. I can't **control** it. I can help take **care** of myself by **communicating** my feelings, making healthy **choices**, and **celebrating** me" (National Association for Children of Alcoholics n. d.). Every one of the Cs is important for adults, too. If you share this message with a child, be sure to also share it with yourself.

Support for Young People

To a child of an addict, silence and isolation can feel like the safest responses to what's happening. But those conditions only serve to worsen the emotional and developmental damage. It's important to let children of addicts to know that there are many other children going through the same experiences—and many young adults who have emerged from them intact. Alateen and Narateen are the two most widely available support groups for the teenage children of addicts. Search the web for meetings in your area, as well as for online chat groups.

Marriages and Partnerships

A marriage or other committed partnership with an addict brings special challenges, whether or not your partner has stopped drinking or using. The advice in this section applies mainly to rebuilding a relationship after the addicted partner has begun the recovery process. If your partner is still drinking or using drugs, the advice in chapters 1 through 6 will be more pertinent.

But don't skip this section just because your loved one isn't sober yet. The guidance here will help you work toward a healthier relationship and a stronger sense of well-being independent of your loved one's current behavior. It can also help you decide whether to leave an addict who is still using or who seems stuck in a cycle of relapse and recovery.

Tough Challenges

Like other family relationships, marriages affected by addiction don't become healthy once the addict has stopped drinking or using. The imbalance inherent in a partnership with an active addict—whose primary devotion was to a substance, not you—often remains. Building a healthier relationship requires work on the part of both partners.

In some cases, a marriage can't survive *without* the addiction. When the huge, shared project of accommodating the addiction comes to an end, the couple discovers that they don't have much else holding them together. Unfortunately, the fear of making such a discovery prevents some people from seeking therapy or other forms of help for their relationship.

Of course, most relationships improve when the addicted partner gets sober, but even these couples bear the scars of the addiction. Old habits die hard. The longer you lived with the addiction, the deeper those grooves will be, and the more effort it will take to escape them. The first step toward doing so is accepting that you can't start over from the point at which the addiction took hold. Healing requires forward progress, not a return to conditions that are irretrievably lost.

Recognize Your Role

In a healthy partnership, each partner contributes more or less equally. With an active addict, that kind of balance is impossible. Practically and emotionally, the substance always comes first, even if the addict would like things to be otherwise. This is the most fundamental obstacle to maintaining a satisfying relationship with an addict.

But in some cases, it's also part of the attraction. Caring for an addicted partner can make you feel extremely useful and needed. For an addict, normal day-to-day functioning—or at least appearing to function—requires a lot of help. That's why many partnerships between a nonaddict and an addict come to resemble the relationship between a parent and child. The non-addict tries to keep the addict out of trouble, takes responsibility for his mistakes, and nurses his wounds.

Some partners of addicts also enjoy the feeling of being perceived as the "good" one—the half of the relationship who is responsible and kind and reasonable. It takes the pressure off any problems the nonaddict may have and provides a built-in excuse for anything that goes wrong. For someone who'd rather not look at her own faults, an addict can, in a way, be an ideal partner. The same goes for someone who, consciously or not, doesn't want the intimacy that a truly committed relationship brings.

All this might not describe you. But it's important to question your role in the relationship and what you've been getting from it. If you don't understand the role you've played, you'll likely continue repeating the same patterns, and the relationship likely won't evolve into a more balanced structure. To start taking a closer look, see exercise 9.

As you explore this issue, you might find that it leads to further questions about the choices you've made and whether they're in keeping with the kind of relationship you'd like to have. Such questions require more extensive, individualized guidance than I can provide here. A skilled therapist can help you untangle these issues and come to a clearer understanding of your needs. Support groups for partners of addicts, which I'll discuss in chapter 9, can also help.

Replacing Old Habits

All partnerships are based, in part, on repetition—it's part of the comfort and familiarity most people seek in a relationship. When entering into a friendship or partnership, we quickly establish norms of behavior. Each person takes on a role.

But relationships with addicts tend to be especially oriented around habits. Drugs and alcohol may promise adventure and excitement, but an addict's life is increasingly driven by repetition—by the daily acquisition and consumption of, and recovery from, his substance of choice. Staying in a partnership with such a person may require the nonaddicted partner to fall into equally repetitive patterns of behavior, such as taking care of the addict, bailing him out of trouble, or even tolerating his abusive behavior.

Quitting these habits cold turkey is much more difficult than replacing them with healthier ones. (Think of a smoker switching to gum or an alcoholic switching to iced tea.) Establishing new patterns takes some effort and repetition, but you can start anytime. Here are some of the most common habits of someone in a relationship with an addict, along with potential replacements.

- *Old habit: Accommodation.* If you've been in a relationship with an addict for a long time, you've likely developed a willingness to overlook some behavior that most people would find unacceptable.

- *New habit: Self-assertion.* Becoming more open and honest with your feelings sounds like a big project, but you can start with a minor shift. When you're uncomfortable, ask yourself why. Express what you find to your partner.

- *Old: Stifling anger.* Being in a relationship with an addict usually entails plenty of anger. If you expressed it every time you felt it, there'd be no time in the day for anything else, so you've likely habitually repressed it.

- *New: Expressing it.* Use the communication strategies described in chapter 3 to begin communicating more honestly about your experience, including negative feelings.

- *Old: Obligations and deals.* Relationships with addicts often involve a lot of promises, deals, and threats, all of which serve as placeholders for normal respect and concern for each other's well-being.

- *New: No strings.* Do and say things because you want to, not because you expect something in return or feel obligated. Similarly, while you can choose to forgive your loved one, she can never "pay you back" for enduring her addiction—that kind of debt breeds resentment, not mutual care.

- *Old: Give and give.* Not expecting much can become so deeply ingrained that it can become hard to accept what's freely offered to you.

- *New: Give and take.* If your loved one offers help or does something considerate or just starts pulling her weight, accept it. Building a more balanced relationship requires you to gladly receive as well as give.

- *Old: Patience.* Patience is a prerequisite for coping with the inconsistent behavior of an active addict. Better days always seem to stay just out of reach.

- *New: Patience.* After being patient so long, the last thing you might want to hear is that *now* you should be patient with the relationship. But if you've stayed in it to this point, waiting out the volatility of early recovery is probably worthwhile.

Don't be surprised if the changes you make, even if they seem small, start to shift the way you feel about yourself and your partner. Combined with all the changes happening for your loved one, that's a whole lot of change. In such a transformative time, it's wise to assume as little as possible. While it's true that the relationship will probably become much more satisfying, it also might look very different from the one you've pictured or hoped for.

Couples Counseling

Most partnerships suffer extreme damage during the course of an addiction. As the addict's unfulfilled promises and unmet responsibilities pile up, so do the partner's grievances and resentments. Professional help can be invaluable in untangling and beginning to deal with all of these problems, as well as in creating a healthier relationship.

Couples counseling won't help much if either partner is still in active addiction. Any competent therapist who identifies addiction in a relationship will recognize that it must be addressed before any significant progress can be made. That's not to say it's pointless to bring an addict to couples counseling. On the contrary, such therapy is often where an addiction is first brought to light—including many cases in which neither partner considered addiction the main source of trouble in the relationship. When the addiction has been treated, and the addict is in active recovery, couples counseling can help the couple repair the damage and start down their new path together.

What If My Loved One Won't Quit?

As we've seen, an active addiction hinders the qualities that enable someone to be a supportive partner. Ending a relationship with an addict may well be one of the best things you can do for your well-being. But in many cases, the decision isn't so simple. Family considerations, religious beliefs, financial constraints, and other factors might influence your decision to stay in a relationship with an addict who is still using.

If you do choose this difficult road, it's important to protect yourself and any children involved. There are some ways of making the best of it:

- *Get help.* The challenges of a partnership with an addict are often too much to handle without professional help. A therapist who specializes in marriage and addiction can help you develop coping skills.

- *Protect children.* If children are present, limit their exposure to the addict as much as possible and communicate regularly with them about what's happening. See "Children and Addiction" above.

- *Address violence.* If physical, verbal, or emotional abuse has happened, it's unlikely to end, even if it lets up from time to time. Leave the relationship if at all possible. Look online for local groups that serve people affected by violence.

- *Be honest with yourself.* Understanding the reasons you choose to stay with the person can help you ensure that you're staying by choice, not out of guilt or fear of the unknown. See exercise 9 at the end of this chapter.

- *Nurture your other relationships.* Many people who realize they're not getting what they need from their partner skip the next step: developing other close relationships with friends and family members.

- *Connect with others in the same boat.* You might feel totally alone, but millions of people are facing similar challenges. Connecting with them can give you a sense of fellowship as well as practical coping strategies. For more information about this, see chapter 9.

- *Revisit your decision.* Check in with yourself periodically to make sure your decision hasn't changed. Staying in a relationship solely out of hope that the addict will change is a recipe for heartbreak. Don't wait and see for the rest of your life.

Embracing Change

Many addicts are surprised to find that recovery—which always seemed boring and safe, just drudgery—can feel more uncertain, more dangerous, and more exciting than their addiction ever was. The people who've been most deeply affected by the addiction often have a similar experience. When the familiar crises and worries and accommodations of an addiction fall away, the addict's loved ones are sometimes at a loss for what to do and even how to feel. This can be disorienting and uncomfortable, and some people respond by returning to the safety of old habits and ways of thinking. Others take it for what it is: a sign of growth and possibility—of new life beginning. The choice is yours.

Looking Toward a New Life

A marriage or other romantic partnership with an addict tends to be oriented toward the addicted partner getting what she wants. In addition to the primary need for the substance, which takes precedence over everything else in the addict's life, the addiction also creates supporting needs—the practical, financial, and emotional help it takes to function and continue using at the same time.

In the presence of all these requirements, the nonaddicted partner's wants and needs tend to take a backseat. As a result, many partners of addicts adjust their expectations, learn to do without some of the normal benefits of a relationship, or begin to deny or downplay their own needs.

To move forward—whether that means trying to heal the relationship or deciding to end it—it's essential to first understand what you've been getting from it. Without this initial step, you're likely to continue getting similar results, whether your partner gets sober or not, or to repeat the same pattern with a new partner.

Exercise 9: Three Questions for Partners of Addicts

Start by answering the following questions in your journal. Doing so can be difficult and uncomfortable, so I've limited the list to three for now. Take your time, and don't worry about writing coherent or convincing responses. Your honesty with yourself is the only requirement here.

- Imagine an alternate reality in which you are never called upon to defend, apologize for, or rescue your partner. Does this sound like a relief, create a feeling of worry, or both? Pay attention not just to your thoughts but also to physical reactions to this prospect, such as tightening up. Why do you think you responded the way you did?

- Think of some of the most stressful events during your loved one's addiction. Leaving aside your feelings toward your partner, ask yourself how you felt about yourself during those times?

- Imagine that your partner asks you to name the three things you want most from the relationship. How does it feel to be asked? Is it difficult to think of three responses? What are they? How does it feel to express them to your partner?

Congratulations on finishing this short but tough exercise. Don't worry if it hasn't yet yielded any new insights. Just by facing these questions, you've made a first step toward a more independent, more satisfying love life. Keep your answers at hand; we'll be delving deeper into these issues in chapter 9. And if you weren't able to complete this exercise, I recommend returning to it after you've read that chapter.

Looking at the Effects of Addiction

Most of us tend to think of addiction as something that affects the addict and the people closest to him. It isn't easy to grasp how an addiction can have a pervasive effect beyond the immediate family. Exercise 10 is designed to help you see, in a simple and memorable way, how addiction has affected your family.

Exercise 10: Visualizing Addiction's Effects on the Family

1. Write the name of the addict in the center of a page of your journal.

2. In a loose circle around the addict's name, write the names of the members of the addict's immediate family.

3. Draw a line from the addict's name to each of the other names. Along each connecting line, write, in a few words, how the addiction has affected that person. (Don't worry about perfect accuracy; if you're not sure, make your best guess.) For example, you might have "Owen," the addict, in the center, with a line drawn to "Grace," his mother, among other names. Along the line to Grace, you might write, "extra stress, anger, gave him money she needed."

4. From each of the names you've written, draw additional lines to the people closest to that person, and add more names, if they're not already on the page. On each connecting line, write the effect. For example, along the line from Grace to her husband, Luis, you might write, "tension, arguments over money."

5. Keep making connections and adding names until you run out of room or names. (If your family is like most with an addiction, the former will happen first.) If the exercise begins to feel overwhelming, put it aside; you can always return to it later.

It can be satisfying or sad—or a little of both—to see so plainly how far addiction's effects radiate. You might find it a relief to see so clearly what you've been feeling the effects of for years.

Note: It might be best to keep your map to yourself, since it includes speculation about other people's relationships. But if you found it helpful, you might want to suggest the exercise to other family members.

Now What?

So far, we've discussed adult addicts and how those addicts affect you and everyone else in your life, including children. But what about addicts who are still children themselves? A lot of the concepts you've learned so far will also apply to dealing with young addicts, but there are also some special factors to consider. For example, teenage addicts are different from a developmental standpoint. Parents of young addicts may also face legal considerations. If you're not dealing with or curious about addiction in children and teens, feel free to skip ahead to chapter 9, which will guide you a couple of steps farther along the path to emotional independence.

CHAPTER 8

The Teenage Addict

My brother and I started out life with different parents. We are siblings through adoption, chosen by a loving couple and raised in a sober household in an upper-middle-class neighborhood. He did well in school and was smart and funny. He excelled in sports. But he also felt a need for attention in order to cover his deep insecurity and the feeling that he didn't really fit in. It was in this search that he discovered cocaine and alcohol. Suddenly he was able to be the person he wanted to be socially. When he was high, he was unstoppable. And when he wasn't, he was constantly trying to re-create that feeling. One night, when he was sixteen, he was dropped off by his friends on the front porch of our house. He was very intoxicated and kept falling down. The next day he was terribly sick, and the mood in the house was heavy. I was fourteen and didn't know how to process this information, but I did know that it was not good. I was afraid for him. That feeling never left me.

Nearly all the challenges we've discussed are magnified when the addict is a young person. Because a teenager isn't yet independent from the family—physically, emotionally, or legally—adolescent addiction hits the whole family much closer to home. The strategies and tools you've learned so far become even more important as you struggle to respond to this particularly painful situation.

But substance abuse by a teenager or child also raises some special concerns. This chapter will address biological, emotional, and practical issues unique to teenage addiction and substance use. Not all of them are gloomy. While most of this book deals with responding to a family member who has become an addict, many adolescents who use or abuse substances haven't yet crossed that line. Learning how to influence those teens to make better decisions can have life-changing results.

Ninety-one percent of people with substance-use disorders started using addictive substances before turning eighteen. Perhaps more alarmingly, 25 percent of people who use such substances as minors go on to develop a disorder, compared to only 4 percent of those who started later (National Center on Addiction and Substance Abuse 2011).

That might sound bleak, but research suggests that counseling for adolescents who are using substances but not yet dependent on them can be very effective. According to one study, substance-using teens who participated in interviews and cognitive behavioral therapy were more likely to abstain than those who did not. And for teens who received enhanced counseling, which included a separate session for parents, the outcomes were even better (Winters et al. 2012). That's why addressing substance use and addiction early and often is so important.

To begin, you have to see your way through all the sadness and fear a young person's substance use can bring. This chapter will help you do that. The guidance here is aimed primarily at parents, but it will also be useful for anyone who is concerned about a young person. And as we'll see, the issues facing young addicts and potential addicts don't expire on the day the person turns eighteen or twenty-one. Their legal status may suddenly change, but their vulnerability and growth continue.

A Brain Under Construction

When teenagers engage in risky behavior like drinking or using addictive substances, exasperated parents often think they are simply "not thinking" or are succumbing to peer pressure. But recent research has shown that adolescents' riskiest behaviors spring from a gap between the maturity levels of two key parts of the brain: the limbic system and the prefrontal cortex. The limbic system, which drives emotion, goes into overdrive in the teenage years. The prefrontal cortex, which governs impulse control and judgment, lags behind, often not reaching full maturity until a person's mid-twenties (Giedd 2015).

I'm sharing this information not for a pop quiz later but because it can help you approach your risk-taking son or daughter with less outrage and more understanding. Teenagers aren't dumb or temporarily insane; they're just wired to take risks. It's important to approach any situation involving teens and substances calmly, with your eyes open, rather than jumping to conclusions. What seems like a dire situation might be a temporary one. Since a teenager's decision-making function is still developing, the risky behavior you're seeing might change entirely in a year or two.

Of course, not all teen substance use stems from a quirk of evolutionary neurology. Teenagers also use substances for the same reasons older people do: to counteract stress, social anxiety, isolation, difficult feelings, loneliness, and boredom. In other words, to meet all the hallmark challenges of the adolescent years. Seen from that angle, it can be surprising that *more* kids don't abuse substances.

That doesn't make the risks any less dangerous. You shouldn't dismiss teenage (or earlier) substance use as experimentation. You should watch for signs of use, ask questions, and respond assertively when you see reason for concern. Most teens who've used substances haven't yet developed the deeply ingrained habits that characterize addiction. There's likely still time for you to make a big difference.

The Harmless-Hardcore Myth

Many parents' approach to teen substance use is based on dividing substances into two vastly different groups: "less harmful" ones (typically alcohol and pot) and "hardcore" drugs (often everything else). Basing your actions primarily on these categories may not be the wisest approach. Any parent should be more concerned about finding a meth pipe than a joint, of course, but you shouldn't focus exclusively on the type of substance. A teenager who has tried a "serious" drug isn't necessarily addicted or even habitually using drugs. Exploration can lead to trying harder drugs even in the absence of a need to escape or self-medicate negative feelings. And substances that some adults consider relatively innocuous *can* be cause for alarm.

On top of those concerns, substance trends are constantly evolving, both in terms of the popularity of different substances and the quality and potency of each substance. That means the drugs that were popular when you were a teen aren't the same ones today's teens are using—even if they go by the same name. In the 1960s, there was marijuana and LSD; in the 1970s, heroin. The 1980s were plagued by cocaine and crack; the 1990s introduced ecstasy. Designer drugs emerged in the 2000s, and by 2010, heroin had made a resurgence.

Today, a typical progression of substance abuse looks like this. A teen starts with the opiate painkillers in his parents' medicine cabinet. As he develops a dependency—and an ever-increasing tolerance—he soon finds that buying opiate pills on the street is far too expensive. Heroin, which is purer and cheaper today than it was in past decades, becomes a more palatable option. (This higher potency has contributed to a sharp rise in overdoses in recent years.)

It's important for parents to also be aware of designer drugs—manufactured substances originally designed to circumvent the legal system. Bath salts (so named for the drug's original packaging, not its chemical content) have gained popularity in some areas. K2, or spice, is a manufactured chemical meant to produce a high similar to that of marijuana. Flakka, a cheap new synthetic drug, has recently been pushed to heroin and crack abusers and is responsible for many violent, psychotic episodes. Note that new designer and synthetic drugs emerge without regulation at first, sold mainly in head shops. They may be at least temporarily legal, until the effects and uses become recognized. This makes them more readily accessible by children. Once enforcement agencies become aware, these drugs are often made illegal.

Another reason for concern, even with substances that are more familiar to adults, is that teenagers don't process them the same way adults do.

Marijuana

The increasing availability and legality of pot hasn't made it less harmful. Studies have shown that marijuana causes more lasting impairments to teenagers than it does to adults. According to neurologist Frances E. Jensen, MD, in her book, *The Teenage Brain*, "Adolescents with only short exposure to cannabis show cognitive deficits similar to those of chronic adult users, but with continued use their cognitive impairment does not completely resolve and in some cases can last for months, even years" (Jensen 2015, 152).

It's also worth considering that today's pot is much stronger than that of previous decades. Back in 1985, THC, the component of marijuana that gets the user high, made up only 4 percent of the average marijuana. By 2009, that figure had risen to nearly 10 percent (Jensen 2015). And a 2015 study of a wide range of legal marijuana available in Colorado found nearly double that amount, 19 percent, with some varieties testing above 30 percent.

Marijuana, in past years, was dubbed a "gateway drug"—a substance that may lead to the use of other illegal drugs. While that statement holds true, it does not necessarily mean that people who smoke marijuana will engage in other substances of abuse. It simply means that the environment of substance use sets the stage for the introduction of other drugs.

Because marijuana lacks some of the addictive qualities that typify other drugs of abuse and causes less intense withdrawal symptoms, its clinical addictiveness has long been debated. There is now little doubt, however, that ongoing use can create lasting physical and psychological changes. "Over time, overstimulation of the endocannabinoid system by marijuana use can cause changes in the brain that lead to addiction," the National Institute on Drug Abuse says (2005, 5). NIDA estimates that 9 percent of people who use marijuana eventually become dependent on it (Anthony, Warner, and Kessler 1994; Lopez-Quintero et al. 2011). That figure nearly doubles—to 17 percent—among those who start using pot in their teens (Anthony 2006; Hall and Pacula 2003). Whatever your opinion on the clinical addictiveness of marijuana, there's no denying that pot now represents a large portion of substance-use problems in the United States. The 2013 National Survey on Drug Use and Health estimated that marijuana accounted for over 60 percent of all cases of illicit-drug abuse or dependence (Substance Abuse and Mental Health Services Administration 2014).

Alcohol

Alcohol, too, has a different effect on teenage brains than on fully mature ones. *The Teenage Brain* describes a catch-22 in which risky behavior such as drinking can stunt the brain development that would lead to less risky behavior: "White matter, the myelin sheaths that help increase the speed and efficiency of information passing through the brain, continues to develop throughout adolescence and well into early adulthood. In teens with alcohol use disorders, the white matter of the corpus callosum, the fibers that connect the brain's two hemispheres and allow them to communicate with each other, becomes damaged" (Jensen 2015, 136).

In an effort to control or monitor their teen's drinking, some parents allow it at home or in certain circumstances. But recent research has found that such an approach can backfire (Trudeau 2010). One study compared parental attitudes toward alcohol during high school to negative experiences with alcohol later on, concluding that "acceptance of underage alcohol use in the home is likely to be an ineffective strategy to reduce the likelihood that one's teen will misuse alcohol in college, while disapproval [of drinking] seems to produce the most optimal outcome" (Abar, Abar, and Turrisi 2009, 545). Knowing where or how your teen uses substances might ease your fears, but it's unlikely to influence him toward healthier behavior.

How Parents Can Respond

All the emotions that come with loving an addict—fear, anger, sadness, helplessness, shame, and guilt—are magnified when the addict or substance abuser is your child. To watch your son or daughter transform from a playful kid into a captive of drugs or alcohol is a uniquely heartbreaking experience.

When your child has been sick, you've given her the medicine or treatment that she needs. But when a child can't stop sickening herself, it's not so simple. It can feel like nothing you do makes a difference. The experience can shake your confidence as a parent. Many parents blame themselves, even those who've done nothing to contribute to the substance use, let alone addiction. "What did I do wrong?" can become an obsessive, unanswerable question. The more urgent question is "What can you do now?"

All the pitfalls of dealing with an addict apply to an addicted teen, too—only more so. Enabling, for example, is especially common among parents of addicts. Young addicts often take advantage of their parents' desire to protect them—and their reluctance to believe the worst—in order to continue using. The tools and strategies described in chapters 1 through 4 can help you to avoid enabling and to maintain firm boundaries. But the challenges parents face demand some additional guidelines.

Adjusting Your Approach

A teenager's substance use might leave you terrified, furious, or even ashamed. Those are all valid reactions. But if they drive your response to the problem, you're unlikely to help as much as you could—and you might even make things worse. If you instead respond in a deliberate, assertive, and loving way, you have a much better chance of influencing your teenager's behavior. How do you get from those raw emotions to this calmer, more effective state?

The emotions can run so high that it's wise to do some preparation on your own or with your partner before you talk to your teenager. Here are five ways to lay the groundwork for a more effective approach:

1. *Step back.* Fear for your child can make you think that you have to react immediately to a new development, such as the discovery of evidence that your child has been using. But you'll rarely be at your most effective in the moments after such an event. Lashing out is unlikely to help. When possible, give yourself time to calm down and discuss the problem with your partner or another loved one before talking to your child.

2. *Pay attention.* Identifying the situation's emotional effects on you can help you avoid succumbing to them. When you find yourself feeling tense, stop for a moment to pay attention to what's going on in your body: Is your jaw clenched? Are you breathing shallowly? Take a moment to name what you're feeling, such as anger, fear, or confusion. Then relax your muscles and take a few deep breaths.

3. *Meet basic needs.* The stress and fear of a child's ongoing substance problem can quickly consume your well-being, leaving you incapable of providing effective help. To counter that, it's essential to get enough sleep, food, and

exercise. Ask your partner or a friend to let you know when you're not doing so.

4. *Get support.* Staying in touch with friends and family is essential during such an unsettling time. Also, talking to other parents who've been through similar situations can provide insight that friends and family cannot; the support groups described in chapter 9 can help. Many parents also find professional help from a therapist or counselor invaluable.

5. *Find ways to relax.* It can feel unnatural or even immoral to enjoy yourself when your child is in trouble. But in order to help your child, you need to be at your best. That means taking time out to unwind and have fun— *especially* if you don't feel like it.

Talking to a Young Substance User or Addict

The techniques you learned in chapters 3 and 4 all apply to teenage addicts. But teenagers do raise some special considerations, especially since so many of them may be in a pre-addiction stage of substance use (to remind yourself of the difference, refer to chapter 1). If that's the case, you might have a lot more power to influence their behavior than you realize. The feeling of "talking to a brick wall" that can typify parenting a teen— especially one who's using substances—is often mistaken. In a national survey of high school students conducted in 2010, 80 percent said their parents' concerns and opinions influence whether or how much they drink or use drugs, and 51 percent said it "very much influences" that behavior (National Center on Addiction and Substance Abuse 2011, 103).

Don't leave the issue alone just because you don't think you're being heard. And don't wait for a problem to progress before addressing it thoroughly and persistently. The earlier someone starts using a substance, the more likely that person is to develop problems with it. For example, one in six of those who started drinking before the age of fifteen eventually meet the clinical criteria for an alcohol-use disorder, compared to only one out of every fifty people who didn't drink until age twenty-one or later (National Center on Addiction and Substance Abuse 2011).

With that in mind, there are best ways to talk to a teen who has shown signs of substance use or addiction:

FRAME YOUR CONCERN CLEARLY

Make it unmistakable to your child that you're raising concerns not to punish him or "set him straight," but because you're afraid for his health and happiness. You've learned what addiction can do, whether you've seen its effect on other loved ones or simply read this book, and you love your child too much not to act on those concerns.

DON'T DEMONIZE SUBSTANCE USE

If your teenager's use of substances has gone beyond a few instances, chances are he uses them in part because they work— that is, they temporarily make him feel better. The more he has enjoyed and valued that effect, the less credible and relatable you'll sound if you label substance use (or users) as stupid or crazy or immoral. Be sure to acknowledge the short-term relief that substances can provide when you discuss the dangers and consequences. The more you appear to "get it," the more likely you are to be heard.

Viewing substance abuse as a misguided attempt to address problems may also enable you to start a conversation about what's bothering your teenager. Focusing too much on the use itself, rather than what's going on with your teen, can mask problems that may be even harder for either of you to talk about, such as depression. A therapist may help draw out these issues if they're present and can help your teen begin learning alternative ways of dealing with emotional discomfort.

Parents often wonder whether they should discuss their own experience with substances with their child. There's no universal answer for this. In some cases, doing so can inadvertently send the message that substance use is okay. But if the child is already aware of your past use, talking openly about your firsthand experience can bolster your authority.

GET PRACTICAL AND SPECIFIC

If your teenager is going to change her behavior in a lasting way, it will be for reasons that matter to her. Any change is less likely to stick if she's doing it only because she thinks you want her to. When you talk about the dangers of substance use, bring the conversation back to activities or goals she cares about that might be incompatible with substance abuse, such as participating in sports, entering a certain profession, or achieving independence.

TEACH BUT DON'T PREACH

Teens might have access to much more information than you did at their age, but that includes vast amounts of misinformation. What they know about substances and addiction is likely to be heavily distorted by friends' anecdotes and pop culture sources. Share what you've learned from this book or from other loved ones' struggles with addiction. Whether or not they ask you for it or seem to welcome it, teens want—and need—reliable information.

DON'T BE DERAILED BY DISHONESTY

Most addicts and substance abusers lie about their use. Teenagers, who are often fearful of consequences and worried about how they're perceived, are even more likely to be dishonest.

When you know or strongly suspect your child is lying, your instinctive response might be to get her to tell the truth before any further conversation can take place. This can lock you into a debate that, like the ones we discussed in chapter 3, doesn't resolve anything. Even if your teen eventually relents, the cross-examination probably won't encourage her to be more open with you in the future.

Instead of taking an accusatory approach, try describing your own experience of what's going on. For example, you might say, "I feel confused and sad, because I smelled pot on you, but you told me that you hadn't been smoking."

To a teenager looking to escape an uncomfortable or scary situation, lying—just like drinking or using—can seem like an expedient solution. As with substance use, it can be helpful to acknowledge that there might be appealing reasons for lying. You might say, for example, "I can imagine why you wouldn't want to share the truth with me, but I want you to feel that you can."

This approach is more likely to encourage a teenager to come clean on his own, helping to create a stronger sense of connection. Even if he doesn't, you don't have to get stuck on the lie. You can keep talking about why you're concerned about what you've observed without attacking him for either the substance use or the dishonesty.

PRACTICE THE ART OF INTRUSION

Teenagers can be notoriously resistant to their parents' questions about how and with whom they're spending their time. But you won't send your child into substance abuse or addiction by making her uncomfortable. Be nosy; ask about friends and plans and contact locations. And keep asking, even when your teenager is irritated by the requests.

This kind of persistence is not to be confused with ignoring your teen's responses, or delivering the same lecture every day. I'm talking about something much harder and more effective:

repeatedly paying attention, listening, and expressing your interest and concern, even when it isn't well received.

Screening and Treatment

If you're concerned about your teenager's substance use, don't hesitate to get professional help. Getting a doctor involved early can demonstrate the seriousness of your concern and can encourage your teen to view substance use as a potentially serious medical matter, not just a bad habit. It's also a good step toward identifying any mental health concerns that may be helping to drive the substance use.

Your child's physician is often the best place to start. Ask the doctor if she can screen for substance abuse using standard assessment tools in order to determine the appropriate treatment (such as therapy or rehab), if any is needed. The doctor might prefer to refer you to an addiction specialist. The website of the American Society of Addiction Medicine can help you find such a specialist yourself. A screening typically involves a series of questions about alcohol and drug use and may also include blood or urine tests (National Institute on Drug Abuse 2014).

Many treatment centers specialize in young addicts or serve them exclusively. A web search for teen treatment centers should provide you with information for any centers in your area. The website of the Partnership for Drug-Free Teens can provide further guidance on recognizing and responding to a teen's substance abuse, connecting with other parents, and finding additional help. You might also check with your child's school. Schools' substance abuse programs vary widely, both in quality and approach; some provide counseling and other nonpunitive help. However, keep in mind that assistance outside the school setting may be preferable, due to the obvious social implications of adolescence.

Carrots and Sticks

When it comes to substance abuse, neither the promise of rewards nor the threat of consequences works as well as they do with some other teenage problems. Threatening to take away the car or phone isn't likely to persuade a substance abuser—let alone an addict—to stop an activity that provides relief, pleasure, escape. Likewise, providing material rewards in exchange for periods of sobriety or participation in treatment will only set the stage for a cycle of substance abuse followed by sobriety-for-hire, rather than lasting recovery.

In addition to not working very well, both prizes and punishments send your teenager the message that recovery is something she has to do for external reasons, rather than wanting to do it so she can live a happier, healthier life. That's why the best reward you can give for moving toward recovery is to support that process with your words and actions. And the most effective threat you can provide is to refuse to support continued substance use.

Legal Considerations

If your child is under the age of majority (eighteen in most states), you can enroll him in rehab without his consent, though it's better if you do get that consent. The more ownership an addict takes of his problem, the more likely he is to recover. That said, it's not true that to get sober, the addict must have that realization *before* entering treatment. Many people achieve long-term sobriety after being effectively forced into rehab, whether the authority was parental, circumstantial, or legal (choosing rehab over jail, for example).

Note that your child also has the right to make some medical decisions without your consent. More than half of the states allow adolescents under eighteen to receive addiction treatment without parental consent. Whether or not parents are notified of such treatment depends on state law (Brooks 1999).

Privacy laws may prevent doctors and other medical professionals—as well as counselors and other addiction-treatment
professionals—from telling you what your child has told them.
Regulations permit disclosure without the adolescent's consent
only in certain situations, such as medical emergencies, risk of
suicide or homicide, child abuse, and necessary communications
among program staff (Brooks 1999). For more information about
your rights and your child's, see the National Institute of Health's
website, at http://www.drugabuse.gov.

The Hardest Decision

If you have an addicted son or daughter who's eighteen or over
who lives with you and doesn't accept treatment, you might eventually face the difficult decision of whether to kick him or her out.
Doing so can go against your parental instincts. Sometimes the
desire to protect and provide for your son or daughter must be
weighed against the safety and well-being of the rest of the family.
In other cases, it can become clear that by continuing to house
the addicted young person, you are enabling the addiction.

I can't make the decision for you, of course, but I can help
you become aware of some factors that can influence your view
of the situation. Before you make a decision, try taking the following five steps:

1. *Set aside guilt.* If you're continuing to provide housing
    because you feel like you're partly to blame for the addic-
    tion—or to make up for past parenting mistakes—try to
    remove that element from your decision making. You
    won't magically stop *feeling* the guilt, but if you let it
    inform your decision, you won't be acting in anyone's best
    interests, including your child's.

2. *Set aside shame.* Another factor that can cloud your per-
    spective is worrying about what other people will think.
    As with guilt, you may still *feel* ashamed, but this decision

is too important to be influenced by your concern for your family's reputation.

3. *Weigh consequences realistically.* The fear of their child living on the streets—or worse—keeps many parents in the position of bankrolling a child's addiction. It's important to remember that an addiction eventually brings dire consequences regardless of where the addict sleeps.

4. *Proximity isn't control.* For many parents, the scariest idea is *not knowing* where their child is. Seeing your child—or knowing where she is—can give you the illusion that you have some control over the situation. If your child is an active addict, you don't.

5. *Don't expect.* Kicking an addict out can protect your family's well-being and let you avoid enabling the addiction. It *might* also help him begin to see the seriousness of his situation. But if you expect that result, you're likely to be disappointed.

Most addicts faced with constant disapproval and demands to enter treatment will eventually remove themselves, not wanting to deal with the repetitive badgering. If your son or daughter doesn't, be prepared for the possibility of enlisting help from law enforcement. Don't hesitate to call the police if you feel any concern for your family's safety. Remember that until your child accepts help for her addiction, any appeasing or compromising support you provide will only prop up her disease. And please keep in mind that many addicts who achieve long-term sobriety view the day they were kicked out as the beginning of the end of their substance abuse.

Resources and Support

Addiction can be an isolating experience for any addict, but especially for a teenager. It's common for teenage addicts who want to get sober to worry that they'll never have fun again. For most of them, substances opened the door to socializing—easing their anxieties and providing a common pastime, or connecting them with a group of kids that they admire—even if it is for the wrong reasons. For some, the idea of hanging out without substances is almost unimaginable.

That's why 12-step programs can be especially effective for young addicts. However, because those programs originated in the 1930s, their tenets can sound archaic to teenage ears. Thankfully, AA, NA, and many other 12-step programs offer meetings just for young people. Hearing other teens openly discuss their struggles can be tremendously reassuring for a newly sober teen who feels doomed to a boring existence. Any visit to a sizable meeting of young addicts generates just the opposite feeling—the energy and vitality of these groups is amazing. (Note that the names of the many different types of 12-step groups can get confusing: Alateen and Narateen, like Al-Anon, are for young friends and family members of addicts.)

A Reminder About Your Well-Being

Any loved one's addiction can consume your well-being. But your child's addiction can do so much faster than any other, quickly damaging your health, relationships, career, and self-esteem. And because parents are *expected* to put their children's well-being first, it can feel wrong to do anything but obsess about your child, long past the point of usefulness. But that's not the best way to help her. The familiar metaphor of the oxygen masks that drop from an airplane ceiling during an emergency has been used to illustrate all kinds of situations. But it fits your situation better than any other: to help your child to the best of your abilities, you have to first make sure that *you* can breathe—that your own needs are met. The first deep inhalation might be painful, but it can also be the beginning of a healthier life.

Back in chapter 4, we discussed how maintaining clear boundaries can protect your well-being. By clearly defining what you will and won't do, boundaries can release you from the guilt, fear, and obligation that can keep you tied to your loved one's behavior. But when the addict or substance abuser is your child, boundaries are more complicated. After all, you're responsible not only for your child's safety and security but also for serving as a positive influence and guide.

But ultimately, you're not responsible for your child's happiness. Accepting this simple concept is difficult for many parents, but it can greatly reduce the torment and indecision that parenting any teen can bring—let alone one who is abusing substances. The more you remind yourself of this concept, the more you'll realize that you can parent more effectively when you accept the limits of your role.

When you stop fighting the unwinnable war of guaranteeing your child's happiness, you'll find you have more energy—and a clearer head—for the tough decisions that you face parenting a teen, including your responses to both positive and negative events. You'll also give your teen a better chance to learn to be responsible and accountable for his own actions. For a young person discovering substances, there's no more important lesson.

Exercise 11: Realize You're Not Responsible for Your Child's Happiness

This simple exercise is designed to help you put this principle into practice and learn how it can help you determine more effective rewards and consequences for your teen's behavior. Use a page or two of your journal to answer these questions:

1. Recall a recent event with your teenager involving substance use. The event can be positive, such as "decided not to join his friends who were smoking pot," or negative,

such as "came home drunk." Describe only the simple facts of the event.

2. Describe your response to the event.

3. How would you have responded differently if you accepted that you weren't responsible for your child's happiness? (Note: If you have trouble with this concept, it can be helpful to imagine how you would respond to a friend's child.)

4. How would this have been more or less effective than your actual response? How might it have changed the message your teen received about his behavior?

There's no correct answer to these questions. But seeing your behavior from a less emotional point of view can give you a glimpse of an approach to parenting that might serve both you and your teenager well in these difficult years.

Now What?

We've done a lot of responding so far—learning to meet challenges with effective strategies, communicating with others more effectively, trying to maximize our helpfulness. But the next chapter is all about you. I'll help you start down the road toward emotional independence—a state in which your well-being won't be tied to the addiction that has captured so much of your time and energy. It won't be easy to get there, but the path isn't as rocky as you might think.

CHAPTER 9

Toward Healthy Independence

Toward the end of my brother's active addiction, my mother and I were faced with a dilemma. By that point, after twenty-plus years of insanity, we had seen the disease for all it was. We had learned how to protect ourselves from his destruction and how to separate enough from him that we could live happy lives. Yet we still loved him, and a time came when we again decided to put his needs ahead of our own. After falling through a glass table, puncturing his lungs, and nearly dying, he'd spent three weeks in the hospital. Now he was being discharged; the tubes were being removed. He'd gone through withdrawal in the hospital and was so weak and physically vulnerable that even homeless shelters wouldn't take him in. It was clear that living on the street would kill him, whether from infection or a return of the pneumonia he had just fought off. So my mom and I chose to help; we made this decision consciously. We safeguarded the house and our possessions, and we created a space for him to come heal, well aware of the risk to ourselves.

So far, this book has concerned itself with answering the most urgent questions you're facing: What's happening to my loved one? What should I do? How can I help? But truly recovering from a loved one's addiction usually requires more than learning how to support her sobriety or help your family heal.

Whether or not your loved one continues to drink or use, the effects of addiction on *you* can be deep and lasting. Addiction can also create and mask emotional problems and harmful mental habits in you, none of which disappear when the addict enters recovery or moves out or leaves your life. The good news is that if you address these challenges actively, they tend to respond very well.

This chapter will help you begin to identify and address these common problems. By the end of the chapter, you'll have made a start toward greater emotional independence—a state in which your peace of mind won't be at the mercy of your loved one's behavior or anyone else's.

What's Wrong with This Picture?

To illustrate the kinds of challenges I'm talking about, imagine this simple scenario (variations of which I've seen too many times to count). A woman suffers for years at the hands of her husband's addiction. All she wants is her husband back—the real one, not the man he's become. She begs him to stop and get help. And then one day, he does. The woman is overjoyed, though worried about relapse. But as he manages to stay sober, her fear gradually fades, and she realizes that she's finally gotten exactly what she wanted. Now that he's sober, she thinks, their relationship will be strong again, and she can finally focus on her own needs and interests, not on shielding their kids from him or cleaning up his messes.

The woman gradually realizes that there's only one problem: she's miserable. Instead of feeling like she's been set free, she's still preoccupied by him and his behavior. When he doesn't behave the way she'd like him to, it irritates her even more than it did in his drinking days. She often finds herself feeling unsure about what to do—and at times, even of who she *is*. And she can't decide what she resents more: what he put her through in his drinking years or all the kudos he's now getting for finally meeting his responsibilities.

You might not experience anything like this. But chances are, if you love an addict, you'll find that recovering from the experience requires more work than you expected. You might also find that in the long run, it's not really about the addict at all. It's about you.

Looking at Yourself

It might not seem important to focus on yourself right now. It might even feel selfish, especially if your family is still struggling to cope with the addiction. But by taking a look at your own needs and challenges now, you'll become better able to handle any challenges that come your way and to lead a happier life, regardless of what your loved one does.

To do so, it's helpful to understand the ways addiction can affect people (beyond the obvious worry and stress and heartache). Caring deeply about an addict can create or deepen unhealthy mental and emotional habits that are hard to break. It can also mask other problems that can prevent you from living a fully satisfying life.

Contingent Happiness

Many people who love addicts learn to embrace an "if only" mindset. To cope with their painful present, they focus on an idealized future. Common thoughts include *If only she'd quit, everything would be okay* and *If only he'd get better, I could do all the things I want to do.* This mental habit places your happiness in the hands of the addict's behavior. That's dangerous, in part because relapse is extremely common. But the subtler and more important problem is that even if your loved one never drinks or uses again, your well-being will still be at the mercy of her behavior, over which you have no control. That's a scary and stressful way to live.

Disguising Other Problems

An addiction also often masks other problems, some of which might have more to do with you than the addict. Some of these problems were caused by the addiction; others may have been present even before the addict or addiction came into your life, but the addiction made them worse. In many cases, especially in romantic partnerships, the addiction may have been part of what subconsciously drew you to the addict. If you've had multiple relationships with addicts or find yourself obsessing about the addict's behavior more than is helpful, it's worth examining whether or not that's a coincidence. To do that, it's helpful to learn about a group of unhealthy traits and habits known as codependency.

Understanding Codependency

Even if you've learned about codependency before, you might not have a firm grasp on what it is. That's because the term has evolved several meanings over the years, all of which are still in use. Accounts of the term's origins differ, but it's fair to say that the concept initially referred to unhealthy attitudes and habits related to being in a relationship with an addict. The term's meaning has since broadened to include a general overreliance on others for one's sense of self-worth. There are almost as many definitions as there are codependent people, but all of them share the same basic idea: a codependent is someone who focuses too much on others, at the expense of his own well-being.

At the core of codependency is the belief that happiness depends on other people, rather than emerging from an innate sense of worth. The central message codependents tell themselves, over and over, is *I am not enough*. In response to that belief, they do everything they can to ensure the approval and affection of other people (sometimes just one person) or to exert control over them. When people don't behave exactly as the codependent would like, he increases his efforts and puts even more effort into bringing about their approval or affection.

What's Wrong with Caring?

Critics of the codependency concept point out the similarities between codependency and normal caring. "Don't we all depend on one another?" they ask. Aren't we wired to care about others and seek affection from them? Isn't selflessness an ideal promoted by just about every spiritual tradition? And don't all loving parents put their children's needs before their own? As Melody Beattie, the best-known author on codependency, puts it, "Sometimes, codependent behavior becomes inextricably entangled with being a good wife, mother, husband, brother, or Christian" (Beattie 2011, 26).

So what distinguishes codependency from a healthy interest in others?

- Codependency is obsessive. The degree of obsession varies widely, but codependency involves out-of-control repetition—returning to the same thoughts and impulses over and over, even when they're not working for you. For example, a codependent may obsessively imagine what another person is thinking, even when doing so never yields positive results.

- For codependents, the urge to feel needed or worthy takes precedence over real care for another person's wellbeing. When others are doing well and don't need help, a codependent person might feel threatened rather than gratified.

- Our natural impulses to concern ourselves with others can normally yield satisfying rewards, such as feelings of togetherness and security. For codependents—even those who have many apparently close and loving relationships—those rewards don't register or don't last for long.

The point isn't that codependency is wrong or weak. It's that it doesn't work. It's a way of living that will keep you in a cycle of constant effort and failure—of trying to control things you can't control and of looking to others to provide a feeling of worthiness that can come only from within.

Codependents and Addicts

Some codependent people repeatedly choose addicts for partners. (Many codependents marvel at their own ability to find—and be attracted to—the one addict in a roomful of people.) You might wonder why, if codependents rely so much on others' behavior and affection, some would choose addicts—people who are, as a group, extremely unreliable. The tendency is easier to understand if you think of it as a compulsion, rather than a true choice. Many of them are stuck in patterns of behavior and thinking they developed in a childhood spent dealing with an addicted parent. A relationship with an addict provides endless opportunities to reenact childhood difficulties, to "fix" unacceptable situations, and to try to control the uncontrollable.

Many codependents didn't grow up in such a household; for them, a relationship based on caretaking or fixing might be primarily a way to avoid self-awareness. The more they focus on someone else, the less they have to take a look at themselves. They fill a role, such as caregiving or victimhood, rather than forming a true intimate partnership. But the satisfaction the role provides is tenuous, since the addict may not always need the person in the same way. It's also deeply unhealthy, since its continuation requires that the addict stay sick.

Recognizing Codependency

Not everyone who loves an addict suffers from codependency. But just about everyone thinks or behaves in a codependent way at some times or with some people. Even if codependency doesn't seem like a big problem for you, identifying it when it arises is a step toward developing a stronger, more independent emotional life.

Examples of codependency range from barely noticeable mental tics to actions that limit or damage your connections with other people. If you're still unsure about what codependency looks like, try this little test: Below are a dozen thoughts and behaviors. Can you pick out the ones that signal codependence?

- You go out of your way to avoid being alone, even for a few hours.

- When you get good news, it doesn't mean anything until you can tell someone about it.

- You often feel responsible for your loved ones' feelings.

- You put your own needs aside to help a loved one "just this once," but it happens over and over.

- You get a quick hit of pleasure from others' praise or affection but soon crave more of it.

- Your sister asks you for a favor that you find unpleasant and would rather not do. You say yes and then think, *Now she owes me.*

- When you're not invited to help, you feel rejected.

- You're often terrified of making a mistake.

- You can't have a good time unless everyone around you is having a good time.

- You often feel compelled to protect people from themselves.

- When you can't seem to influence or help someone, you just try harder.

- You often do too much for someone—or get too involved—and then pull back to the other extreme and cut that person off.

If you said these are all common signs of codependency, you're right. And if you recognize some of them in yourself, it's a great idea to investigate codependency further and to try some of the suggestions and exercises that make up the rest of this chapter.

Self-Care

Learning to take care of yourself doesn't require you to become entirely self-sufficient. Everyone needs connections with other people. It does require you to discover and reinforce ways you can find peace of mind regardless of how others are treating you at any given moment. As Melody Beattie puts it, "If you want to get rid of [codependency], *you* have to do something to make it go away. It doesn't matter whose fault it is. Your codependency becomes your problem; solving your problems is your responsibility" (2011, 20).

If you've been focused on an addicted loved one for long, your self-care muscles likely need some exercise. Here are a few ways to start working them out.

Shake Things Up

Changing the way you think and feel won't happen overnight, but you can start changing what you *do* right away. Interrupting familiar routines that don't energize you can help accelerate the more profound changes and can help you feel better while they're happening. One way to break up familiar patterns is to go out of your way to do things for yourself—treating yourself to activities or events or hobbies that don't depend on pleasing, entertaining, or impressing anyone else. If you don't like to fly solo, invite a friend along. Just make sure you're doing it because *you* want to.

Take the Do-Nothing Challenge

If codependency is a problem for you and someone you love is suffering, one of the hardest and most rewarding things you can do is nothing. Letting someone learn from a mistake, rather than giving in to the urge to insert yourself into the situation, is often the most loving choice. It shows your loved one that you respect her ability to find her own way and that you also respect the limits of your own power. Inaction takes practice—sometimes a lot of it. Watch for opportunities to support someone by deciding not to try to solve her problems.

Get Moving

You don't need to join a gym or hire a personal trainer to get substantial emotional benefits from exercise. Focus on regularity, not intensity, and try to get outside if you can, especially if you spend most of your day sitting in front of a screen. Of course, if you're the kind who loves to blow off steam with an intense spinning session, go for it. But now's a great time to try a new sport or movement-oriented activity you've been curious about, like dance, yoga, or cycling. Or start walking daily, even if it's just around the block.

Create

Creativity can be a way to communicate, but it's also a way to strengthen your sense of who you are, no matter what it is that you're making. If you're like many people, it's hard to separate creating anything from other people's evaluations and judgments. Try writing, drawing, cooking, crafting, or building something no one will ever see.

Consider Your Own Substance Use

As we've seen, dealing with an addict can be stressful and discouraging. Sadly, one of the easiest, most accessible ways to cope with loving an addict is to use substances yourself. They often provide temporary shelter from the tough, complicated emotions brought by loving an addict. And because you have an addict to measure yourself against, it can be much easier to downplay your use. "I might overdo it now and then," many loved ones of addicts say, "but I'm nothing like him." That's a dangerous way to measure whether your own substance use has become a problem, since substances affect everyone differently.

What's a better way to gauge your use? If you're wondering if you might be becoming dependent, try limiting your intake. Use the substance moderately (two drinks, for example) and then stop. If you fail to do so—or if stopping is difficult or makes you miserable—that's cause for concern. Talk to a therapist, doctor, or one of the support groups described in chapter 6, in the section "Ongoing Treatment and Support."

Reflect

If you're part of—or even just interested in—a spiritual tradition, try spending some regular time with it. A sense of connection with something larger or more lasting than yourself can be a great help as you seek more reliable sources of serenity than the shifting affections of others. Meditation, prayer, and ritual can also provide relief from overthinking and worry. Don't worry if you're not "doing it right" or believing what you think you should believe. Just give it a shot.

Getting Support

Ironically, developing your capacity for self-care is much easier done with the help of others—professionals as well as people who have struggled with the same experiences.

How Therapy Can Help

Many people who've been focused for a long time on an addicted partner struggle to even name their own needs, let alone know how to go about filling them. They may even balk at the idea of thinking about what they need; the idea can seem selfish or indulgent or even ridiculous. It's common for an overwhelming need for approval to get tangled up with healthier needs for supportive connections with other people. A therapist can be invaluable in drawing out these threads.

Professional help is also important to identify and address unresolved problems from childhood that still influence your behavior. Some codependents find it necessary to address these problems before their habitual focus on caring for and controlling others can change.

A therapist can help you uncover the sources of unhealthy behavior and begin to develop new habits of thinking and behavior that promote self-care. Methods vary, but most skilled therapists can help you develop tools for building your self-esteem and developing healthier relationships.

Support Groups

Four major groups serve people affected by relationships with addicts. All four function like AA in that they're based on the 12 steps and offer meetings supported by small, voluntary donations from their members.

- Al-Anon is the oldest and largest group. It started when wives of AA members saw that AA was working for their husbands but not addressing their own experiences and frustrations. They adapted the 12 steps for their own use, and now Al-Anon is nearly as widespread as AA itself.

- Nar-Anon, as you might have guessed, is like Al-Anon but meant for those who have been affected by others' drug addictions, rather than alcoholism.

- Codependents Anonymous, or CoDA, is similar in many ways to Al-Anon and Nar-Anon. But CoDA groups tend to focus more on the difficulties of sustaining healthy relationships in general than on the particular challenges of loving an alcoholic or addict.

- Adult Children of Alcoholics (ACOA) addresses many of the same challenges as the other groups but is aimed at helping people recognize and repair the damage caused by a dysfunctional childhood. Despite its name, not all members of ACOA had alcoholic or addicted parents; some members experienced other forms of neglect or abuse that have led to similar problems.

If you're interested in getting support and guidance and fellowship from people who are actively addressing their codependency, I encourage you to try a few meetings in your area. Some people will quickly find a strong preference for one group; others are members of multiple groups. Within each of these groups, the format and tone can vary greatly from one meeting to the next. For example, some are more spiritually oriented than others. A quick Internet search should turn up numerous options. If you live in a remote area or don't want to meet with others in person, the groups offer online meetings.

For those opposed to 12-step programs, it can be frustrating to learn that 12-step groups are the only game in town in many areas. If you know you don't want to attend a 12-step group, your local options may be limited, and you may have to rely on online groups. Note, however, that some therapists lead group therapy sessions focusing on issues related to loving an addict.

Why to Stick with It

Replacing a mindset that took years to develop won't happen overnight. It also won't be easy. Taking an honest look at yourself—and then taking action—requires courage and persistence. But the potential rewards are enormous, and they can start showing up right away. Before long, you might learn that you're capable of a contentment much deeper and more durable than the provisional happiness you've settled for in the past. Or you might just find yourself enjoying things a little more and worrying about them a little less. In either case, you're worth the effort.

Victims

Earlier in this chapter, I described the caregiver role that many people play with addicted loved ones. An equally common role is victim. In a way, it's just the other side of the coin: both of these roles free you from responsibility. Your problems are caused by the addict (or others), and there's nothing you can do about them. That might sound negative, but during troubling, painful times, it can feel like a great relief. That's why just about all of us fall into a victim mindset now and then.

Victimhood often doesn't look the way you might expect. A stereotypical victim goes around complaining about her problems to anyone who'll listen, but many people stuck in this role demonstrate no such behavior. Their victimhood is more a matter of repeating the same resigned thoughts to themselves, regardless of what's actually happening. Whether you have these thoughts continuously or just occasionally, recognizing them and considering alternatives is a big step toward getting unstuck.

Exercise 12: Beyond Victimhood

On a page of your journal, create three column headings: *Event, Victim View,* and *Healthier View.*

In the *Event* column, briefly describe an upsetting recent incident or conversation. Under *Victim View,* interpret it in the most victimized way possible—focusing on the other person and the harm she's done to you. In the *Healthier View* column, try to come up with an interpretation that replaces blame and powerlessness with an idea of what you *can* do.

Event

Marlene missed her brother's graduation.

Victim View

She knew how important this was to him and to me. I'm sure she was just getting high with that guy again. Now I have to make up some lie to cover for her. I don't even know why I thought she'd show up—every time something good happens she finds a way to ruin it.

Healthier View

I'm so proud of our son and so glad to have shared the day with him. It's sad that Marlene missed out on a great event. She knows I'll support her recovery if she chooses to get help.

Don't worry if you don't fully believe the healthier view. The idea here isn't to force yourself to think a certain way, but to notice that there are alternatives to a victim-oriented interpretation of a difficult event. Note also that refusing to be a victim doesn't mean you suddenly stop being hurt by your addicted loved one or others. It means that your life isn't *defined* by that harm— or by anything someone else does. Try this exercise whenever you're disappointed in someone.

Beyond Obsessive Thinking

Codependency relies on obsessive thinking. If we didn't repeat the same habitual negative thoughts, over and over, we wouldn't repeat the same ineffective actions. But the problem isn't the thoughts themselves. It's that we get so caught up in them.

One way to develop your resistance to these thoughts is meditation. Many people resist meditation after finding that it doesn't immediately yield the serenity they think they're supposed to be feeling. "I tried it, and it's not for me," they say. "My mind was just racing the whole time!" That's actually a sign that meditation might work especially well for you. The more frenetic your thinking, the more relief you stand to gain when you achieve some distance from it. And you don't have to spend hours a day with it or sit on the floor cross-legged or take part in any unfamiliar rituals to see benefits.

Exercise 13: Letting Your Thoughts Pass You By

Try this simple exercise:

1. In a quiet room, sit upright on a chair or cushion. Use cushions or supports as needed to make yourself comfortable—or even lie down, if you can do so without drifting off to sleep.

2. Set a timer for five minutes.

3. Close your eyes. Breathe in through your nose. Listen to the sound your breath makes.

4. Count your breath silently to yourself. Say "one" on the inhale and "one" on the exhale, then "two" on the next inhale and then "two," "three" and then "three," and so on.

Don't try to breathe in any special way, just listen to your breath as you count.

5. Whenever a thought pops up, just notice it. Don't try to shut it down or avoid it. Some of these thoughts might be the kind we've discussed in this chapter, such as worrying about what others are doing or thinking, but they can be about anything. You might find yourself irritated by the neighbor's dog barking outside or thinking about how cute your new nephew is or replaying a conversation from last night or planning tonight's dinner menu or noticing that your ankle hurts.

6. Whatever the thought is, picture it as a bubble floating up and away or as a leaf floating by in a stream. Again, you're not doing anything *to* the thought. You're just observing it as it goes by.

7. When the thought has passed, return to counting your breaths, starting at one again. If you make it to ten, start at one again. Repeat until the alarm sounds.

If you found this experience too intense, start with a shorter length of time—even one minute—or try it with your eyes open, though don't look around the room. Note that if you found the practice not merely uncomfortable but deeply disturbing, please contact a mental health professional.

The more routine your meditation practice is, the more effective it will be. As you continue, try extending it by a minute or two each week. Most people who meditate regularly find that it doesn't completely eliminate negative or habitual thoughts. Instead, they find themselves less likely to be driven by those thoughts throughout the day. That might not sound like much, but it's a profound shift away from unproductive cycles and toward a much wider world of choice and possibility. In other words, please give this a try! You deserve the rewards it can bring.

Now What?

In this chapter, we learned how a loved one's addiction can affect your own emotional life and mask problems. We identified habits that can hold your well-being hostage to others' unpredictable behavior. We also discussed some ways to challenge those habits and begin to forge a freestanding sense of self-worth. In the final chapter, we'll set the stage for your ongoing journey, including the most important principles for lifelong recovery. You'll also learn how to continue supporting your loved one's sobriety, even after a relapse. I'll show you what's ahead, some of the best ways to get there, and what to do when you find yourself heading in the wrong direction.

CHAPTER 10

Recovery for Life

Fifteen months have passed, and my brother is now truly clean and sober. He finally listens to what he's told and lives according to what he has learned in his years of treatment. He belongs to a 12-step fellowship. He has a sponsor, he has friends, and he has a life that is now beginning. He's going to school to become a drug and alcohol counselor.

I have my brother back, my mother has a son, and we have desperately missed him. When I look at my big brother now, I'm sure that anyone watching us can see the pride on my face. I believe that he was saved by a combination of exhaustion, love, perseverance, and knowledge.

A part of me will always be hypervigilant when it comes to him. A certain tone in his voice will create a reaction of panic in me, and I'll ask him what's wrong. It gets easier with time. I am grateful for the time I have with him now, and I cherish every day, taking it one day at a time. I know that this time with him may someday end, although I pray it does not.

Because we've covered a lot of ground in this short book, I want to make sure you don't lose sight of the basics—the concepts that will serve you and your family for the rest of your lives. Responding to addiction is often difficult and uncomfortable, but once you accept a few fundamental principles, it doesn't have to be complicated. These principles might not always be easy to live by, but they are simple:

- Addiction is not curable, but it is highly treatable.

- You can't treat your loved one's addiction.

- The best way to assist your loved one is to support his efforts to get treatment and help from professionals and peers.

- You can help your loved one, but you can't control his thinking or behavior.

- Whatever your loved one does, you can live a life that doesn't depend on his current condition or behavior.

The first principle is the most important. It's essential not to lose sight of what addiction is. It's not a bad habit, a moral failing, or a temporary problem that goes away when the addict quits. It's a progressive and incurable illness that needs to be treated. Many people who accept this concept during a crisis gradually lose sight of it after their loved one stays sober for a while. Everything seems fine, and their loved one isn't drinking or using, so it's easy to start thinking the addiction has been cured.

That's a serious mistake for a couple of reasons. First, you can still influence your loved one. If you see that he's not getting treatment and support for his addiction and say something, you might help him avoid going down a path that leads to relapse. Second, if your loved one does drink or use again, it might not be treated by you or other family members as the emergency that it is, especially if his use is moderate at first. (In my experience, it doesn't take long after a relapse for most addicts to get themselves into worse shape than ever.)

I hope you don't take this reminder to mean that you need to expect the worst, that you will always be waiting for the other shoe to drop. Many of us have learned to take exactly the opposite lesson from this unpredictability and lack of control: to treat it as motivation to focus on what we *can* control.

Your Loved One's Changing Journey

Every addict's recovery is different. Your loved one might find that a support program replaces the feelings of relief and community that she'd always sought from drugs and alcohol. She might find that therapy or a spiritual practice reduces her urge to self-medicate. And she might even manage to quit for good without any ongoing treatment or support. (That tends to be a much harder and lonelier way to go, for both the addict and anyone who cares about her, but it does happen.) And she might relapse, once or many times, with or without warning signs.

That doesn't mean that nothing you do matters. Continuing to support your loved one's recovery begins with continuing to pay attention to how she's doing. Many addicts focus less on recovery the longer they stay sober. Their attention turns to the ordinary challenges and responsibilities of life. That's wonderful, but it can be dangerous if they don't keep up the treatment and support that got them this far.

It's very common for addicts to prematurely feel like they get it and start prioritizing things other than their sobriety. While it may be true that they don't need as much intensive support and treatment as they did in their first weeks and months, I've also found it to be true that those who stop actively working toward their recovery are much likelier to relapse.

What to Watch For

If you choose to continue actively supporting your loved one's recovery, you should never consider her addiction resolved. It's entirely possible to relish the changes that her sobriety has brought to your family without turning a blind eye to signs of trouble. Beyond obvious red flags such as hanging out with old drug-using friends or quitting a support program, there are a few common developments worth watching for:

- *Too good to be true.* Addicts who seem to go out of their way to reassure you of how well they're doing—or who downplay or deny their struggles—are often setting themselves up for relapse, even if they truly believe they're doing as well as they claim to be doing.

- *Old patterns return.* Patterns associated with substance use often precede a return to the use itself. For example, a drug addict might become secretive even before he has anything to hide. An alcoholic might go to a bar without drinking. Both can be cases of the addiction paving the way for a return to active use.

- *Resignation.* Addicts tend to struggle to adjust to life without their substance. That's true even for many of those who actively work at their recovery every day. So an addict who's having a hard time isn't necessarily in trouble. But resignation is another matter. Statements of hopelessness or indifference like "What's the point?" often signal a return to addictive thinking, which can lead quickly to relapse.

Another precursor to relapse isn't so much behavioral as circumstantial, but it's common enough to warrant special mention. Pain medication, even when legitimately prescribed to the addict, should be approached with extreme caution, whether or not the addict is primarily addicted to a similar substance. That means avoiding it, if possible, and taking it only as prescribed and only for as long as it is needed. Supervision of the medication is always a wise choice and a smart way to ensure the proper use and intension of the medication.

What You Can Do

Please remember that your loved one's continuing sobriety is ultimately up to him. If you decide that after helping him enter recovery once or twice, you've spent enough time and energy on the problem, that's an entirely valid choice. But if you'd like to continue supporting his recovery, there are ways to help without risking your own well-being.

The techniques and strategies you learned in chapter 6, "Supporting Your Loved One's Recovery," will come in handy whenever your loved one seems to be struggling or neglecting his recovery. I hope you'll revisit that chapter, including the relapse response plan you created (exercise 8). Additionally, there are three habits that are particularly helpful for dealing with an addict over the long term: noticing and commenting, restating your position, and living your life.

NOTICE AND COMMENT

Many family members tiptoe around their sober loved one. As long as she's not drinking or using, the reasoning goes, let's not do anything to upset her. That approach can contribute to the feelings of isolation a struggling addict is likely feeling. And you can express concern without coming across as a nag or narc. Frame it in terms of your own specific observations ("I'm worried, because I noticed that you stopped hanging out with your sober friends"), rather than judgments ("You're so irritable lately") or blame ("You're driving me crazy") or orders ("You need to get to a meeting"). Review chapter 3 for a refresher course on communicating your concern.

RESTATE YOUR POSITION

Some addicts who are nearing relapse—and especially those who have already relapsed in secret—feel a strong sense of shame and may be extremely hesitant to ask for help from those who've done so much already. If you're willing and able to help, let your loved one know, while also indicating the limits of your help. (Revisit chapter 4 for why and how to set strong boundaries.) For example, you might say you'd be happy to help your loved one find a new therapist or go back to rehab or 12-step meetings, but you won't let her stay with you. Reiterating your willingness to help *and* your need to protect yourself can clear the air for both of you.

LIVE YOUR LIFE

Don't let your loved one's situation define yours. This doesn't mean going on about your business and pretending not to care that something scary might be happening again. But it's important to demonstrate to yourself and other family members that your loved one's addiction isn't calling the shots. In a true emergency, you might *choose* to interrupt your life to support your loved one. But even then, you don't have to obsess about his situation. Don't neglect your other relationships or any other support that you've been getting. Most importantly, remember that whether and how you help is always up to you.

Coming to Terms with Relapse

For addicts, relapse is the norm, not the exception. That's not to downplay its seriousness; any relapse can have dire consequences. But it's important to know that relapsing is something that most addicts do—and that you can't prevent it by being perfectly supportive. If your loved one relapses, it doesn't mean that you've failed or that your loved one is weak or stupid or suicidal or doomed. It means that he's an addict.

A return to drinking or using can be confusing and scary for everyone who cares about your loved one. But it's usually not the end of the story. I know countless addicts who relapsed many times before achieving what turned out to be long-term sobriety.

A relapse can be especially baffling and painful for you if your loved one seemed to get it—to understand the importance of staying sober and to see the wreckage it has caused. This can be so disheartening that you might be tempted to take it to mean that he'll *never* recover. But again, the only thing it means for sure is that he's an addict. And that he has more work to do.

Opting Out

Most of this book has been concerned with how to help your loved one. But for many of us, the more pressing question at some point becomes *whether* to continue helping an addicted loved one—or to cut all ties with him. In some cases, the only way to achieve healthy independence is to remove yourself completely from the addict's life.

Only you can decide when it's time to do so, but some simple guidelines can help. There are a number of circumstances in which you should seriously consider breaking contact with your loved one:

- You've been subjected to or have begun to fear emotional or physical abuse.

- When you try to help, you feel resentful, not helpful or hopeful.

- You can't seem to interact with your loved one without reverting to unhealthy patterns of behavior, or you no longer trust yourself when it comes to dealing with her.

- You've considered your options and want to see how distancing yourself from the addict changes your experience of life.

Note that "your loved one keeps relapsing" isn't on this list. That's because such a situation is all about your loved one's behavior, not your well-being. If your loved one keeps relapsing *and* your feelings about the situation are preventing you from finding happiness, that's another matter. Also, note that an addict needn't be actively using to present problems; some can be more difficult to deal with when they're without their substance of choice.

The decision to distance yourself can be a painful one for everyone involved. Before settling on a choice, you might want to discuss the situation with a therapist or trusted friend. But please keep in mind that, ultimately, your reasons don't have to suffice for anyone but you.

If you do decide to break ties, I encourage you to do it simply. A long, emotional letter listing all your justifications for doing so is not a break. It's a continuation of your attempts to communicate with and possibly influence your loved one. A break is best expressed simply, and in the past tense. Short, irrefutable statements of fact, such as "For my own reasons, I've decided not to be in contact with you" or "I can no longer participate in your life" neither add unnecessary drama nor keep the door open for future discussion. By contrast, statements like "I'm never speaking to you again" or "I'm out of your life forever" are arguable predictions that can needlessly intensify a volatile situation.

Keep in mind that in potentially abusive situations, it may be best not to communicate even such a simple message. It's not your responsibility to keep your loved one informed of the way you choose to lead your life. Talk to a police officer, counselor, or lawyer about the safest ways to proceed, and establish an emergency plan with supportive people in case you need to quickly leave an unsafe environment.

Also keep in mind that if you decide to end your relationship with the addict, your decision does not have to be forever. Situations can change. When a different scenario presents itself, you may have the opportunity to change your mind. But—and this is very important to remember—the opportunity to rethink your decision must be initiated by the addict, *not* you. Your loved one should be in long-term recovery, and her motivations should include nothing other than pure remorse and her desire to make amends. If this happens, you will need to reexamine the pros and cons of the new circumstances, as well as the risks involved. This choice is very personal; there is no right or wrong. You might choose to reengage. Or you might stand by your decision to stay out of her life. If you choose to accept her amends or choose for-giveness, know that it does not imply that everything is okay and forgotten. It also doesn't imply that your boundaries will change.

You're Not Alone

Another basic concept I want to leave you with has nothing to do with your loved one. Almost every difficulty described in this book can be eased by sharing it with others. Reaching out to those who've gone through similar struggles, inside and outside of your family, is one of the most powerful things we can do in the face of addiction.

Unfortunately, doing so doesn't come naturally to many of us. We are embarrassed or fear that our troubles won't measure up to what other people have endured or that our story is too awful to inflict on anyone else. Or that there's no point, since we've read all about addiction and we know what to do.

But learning about addiction and the smartest ways to deal with it can do only so much. Fellowship with others who are in the same boat can turn those concepts into something you really get, at a gut level. More importantly, sharing your experience can dramatically lighten your emotional load. You might not realize how much of the pain you've experienced comes from feeling like you're the only one going through it.

That's why I encourage you to check out at least one of the support groups I've mentioned in this book. If the idea of getting help from strangers doesn't appeal to you, try thinking of it the other way around: as a way to be of service to them. Simply sharing your story with others who are struggling can transform your difficulties into a gift for others—and for yourself. It's just about impossible to feel bad while you're helping someone else. (For me, the process of writing this book has been proof of that concept.) Seeing how your own story can help someone else is an experience not to be missed. And it's one you richly deserve.

We're Just Getting Started

My brother and I are both doing great today. And by "today," I don't mean some vaguely defined present moment. I mean literally in this moment, at 6:07 on a summer evening, as I type these words.

I can't say that I'm grateful for everything he and I have been through. But I can say that the experience has led me to grow as a person and a professional. It's made my bonds to my family stronger than ever. It has inspired me to meet and try to help a lot of wonderful people facing similar struggles. And it's led me to a new perspective on life—not that I asked for one—in which my own sense of worth and well-being don't depend on anyone else's behavior. Finally, it's given me a new appreciation for what I have right now, as well as a healthy aversion to dwelling on the past or speculating about the future.

I don't know how or what my brother will be doing in a month or a year or ten years. I do know that I have the tools to respond to whatever happens and that I can always choose to live my own life to the fullest. And I know in my bones that I'm not alone. I hope that after reading this book, you feel the same way.

We're nearing the end of our time together, at least for now. But your recovery is just getting started. And in truth, so is mine. All we have is today. And that's plenty.

Control

You've probably heard the Serenity Prayer. Popularized by 12-step groups, it's now showing up all over the place, from pop songs to bumper stickers. It goes like this: "God, grant me the serenity to accept the things I can't control, the courage to change the things I can, and the wisdom to know the difference."

Whatever you think about the "God" part of the prayer—or even about the idea of praying in the first place—learning and embracing the distinction between what you can and can't control can be tremendously powerful. This exercise will give you practice in doing just that.

Exercise 14: Control

Use a page of your journal to create a table with three columns, with the headings *Topic*, *I Can Control*, and *I Can't Control*. In the first column, write a topic that's been on your mind, such as a person, event, or conflict. Under *I Can Control*, list things related to that topic that are within your power. Under *I Can't Control*, list things that aren't.

For example, if you write the name of your sister, Lucia, in the topic column, the column of things you can control might include "What I say to her" and the corresponding thing you can't control might be "How she responds." And then continue, and note that the *Control* column doesn't always have to have a counterpart in the *Can't Control* column (and vice versa):

Lucia:

I Can Control	I Can't Control
"Whether I help her again."	"Her gratitude or lack thereof."
"How I help, if I do."	"My past actions toward her."
	"Her recovery."

Tomorrow night's party:

I Can Control	I Can't Control
"Whether to go."	"What anyone else there does."
"When to leave."	"How much anyone drinks."
"Whether to talk to Jay."	"How the party will go."

Keep going as long as you like, with as many topics and as many related elements for each, as you like.

Exercise 14 can be especially useful when you're anticipating an uncomfortable or highly emotional situation. But some people find it useful to do on a daily basis. It can be a great relief to remind yourself that you aren't pulling the strings.

Gratitude

You've done some difficult work in this book, including some challenging examinations of your loved one, your family, and yourself. I want to end on a brighter note. This final exercise is one that's worth repeating whether or not addiction continues to be a big part of your life. And it couldn't be much simpler.

Exercise 15: Gratitude List

Each day, write down three things you're grateful for.

Don't worry if your list doesn't sound impressive or profound or if it mixes big things (good health) with small ones (good coffee). In fact, one benefit of this exercise is that it can help you develop appreciation for things we normally take for granted.

Repeat the exercise daily, and see how long you can go without repeating an item from a previous day. Ask a friend to join you, and exchange lists every day by text, e-mail, or phone. Or just use your journal and keep your list to yourself. Either way, this exercise can help you see addiction as just one part of your life. Reminding yourself of all the things that bring you joy and satisfaction can help you stay balanced through easy and tough times alike.

The point isn't to count your blessings or to force yourself to be glad that things aren't worse. It's to develop your appreciation of all the gifts of your life and to avoid fixating on your challenges. Try it for a couple of weeks and see if you like the changes it brings. If you do, there's no reason to stop.

Now What?

Your journey toward a more independent and satisfying life is under way. I hope that your loved one's recovery has also come a long way, and I hope you'll come back to this book and its exercises whenever things don't feel quite right. Or even when they do. I hope that it's a guide you keep close by as your family's recovery continues.

But I also hope that you'll treat it as a launching pad, not just an instruction manual. Exploring the concepts, support groups, and other resources described throughout this book might yield benefits well beyond the help they provide to deal with a difficult family situation. Who knows? A few years from now, you might find that meeting the challenge of your loved one's addiction transformed your life for the better.

Whether that happens or not, I hope you won't get too discouraged when things feel like they're not getting better. For most of us, loving an addict is a rollercoaster, not a steady ascent. If you find yourself falling back into old habits and patterns, it doesn't mean you've lost all the progress you've made. Instead, take it as a reminder to get back to doing the things that worked for you early on.

The 12 Steps of Alcoholics Anonymous

1. We admitted we were powerless over alcohol—that our lives had become unmanageable.

2. Came to believe that a power greater than ourselves could restore us to sanity.

3. Made a decision to turn our will and our lives over to the care of God as we understood him.

4. Made a searching and fearless moral inventory of ourselves.

5. Admitted to God, to ourselves, and to another human being the exact nature of our wrongs.

6. Were entirely ready to have God remove all these defects of character.

7. Humbly asked Him to remove our shortcomings.

8. Made a list of all persons we had harmed, and became willing to make amends to them all.

9. Made direct amends to such people whenever possible, except when to do so would injure them or others.

10. Continued to take personal inventory and when we were wrong, promptly admitted it.

11. Sought through prayer and meditation to improve our conscious contact with God, as we understood Him, praying only for knowledge of His will for us and the power to carry that out.

12. Having had a spiritual awakening as the result of these Steps, we tried to carry this message to alcoholics, and to practice these principles in all our affairs.

References

Abar, C., B. Abar, and R. Turrisi. 2009. "The Impact of Parental Modeling and Permissibility on Alcohol Use and Experienced Negative Drinking Consequences in College." *Addictive Behaviors* 34: 542–47.

Alcoholics Anonymous. 2001. 4th ed. New York: Alcoholics Anonymous World Services.

American Society of Addiction Medicine. 2011. *Public Policy Statement: Definition of Addiction.* http://www.asam.org/docs/publicy-policy-statements/1definition_of_addiction_long_4 –11.pdf?sfvrsn=2.

Anthony, J., L. A. Warner, and R. C. Kessler. 1994. "Comparative Epidemiology of Dependence on Tobacco, Alcohol, Controlled Substances, and Inhalants: Basic Findings from the National Comorbidity Survey." *Experimental and Clinical Psychopharmacology* 2: 244–68.

Anthony, J. C. 2006. "The Epidemiology of Cannabis Dependence." In *Cannabis Dependence: Its Nature, Consequences and Treatment*, edited by R. A. Roffman and R. S. Stephens. Cambridge: Cambridge University Press.

Beattie, M. 2011. *Codependent No More.* Center City, MN: Hazelden.

Briggs, B. 2015. "Colorado Marijuana Study Finds Legal Weed Contains Potent THC Levels." NBC News. March 23. http:// www.nbcnews.com/storyline/legal-pot/legal-weed-surpris ingly-strong-dirty-tests-find-n327811.

Brooks, M. K. 1999. "Legal and Ethical Issues," in Center for Substance Abuse Treatment's *Treatment of Adolescents with Substance Use Disorders*, Treatment Improvement Protocol (TIP) Series, No. 32. Rockville, MD: Substance Abuse and Mental Health Services Administration. http://www.ncbi .nlm.nih.gov/books/NBK64357.

Brunette, M. F., K. T. Mueser, and R. E. Drake. 2004. "A Review of Research on Residential Programs for People with Severe Mental Illness and Co-occurring Substance Use Disorders." *Drug and Alcohol Review* 23: 471–81.

Dayton, T. 2006. "The Set Up: Living with Addiction." Rock- ville, MD: National Association for Children of Alcoholics. http://www.tiandayton.com/wp-content/uploads/2013/03 /The-Set-Up-Living-With-Addiction.pdf.

De Leon, G. 2010. "Is the Therapeutic Community an Evidence- Based Treatment? What the Evidence Says." *International Journal of Therapeutic Communities* 31: 104–28.

Dennis, M. L., M. A. Foss, and C. K. Scott. 2007. "An Eight-Year Perspective on the Relationship Between the Duration of Abstinence and Other Aspects of Recovery." *Evaluation Review* 31: 585–612.

Giedd, J. N. 2015. "The Amazing Teen Brain." *Scientific Ameri- can*, 312: 33–37.

Hall, W. D., and R. L. Pacula. 2003. *Cannabis Use and Depen- dence: Public Health and Public Policy*. Cambridge: Cambridge University Press.

Horvath, A. T., K. Misra, A. K. Epner, and G. M. Cooper. 2005–2015a. "Drug Seeking and Cravings: Addictions' Effect on the Brain's Reward System." http://www.communitycounsel ingservices.org/poc/view_doc.php?type=doc&id=48375 &cn=1408.

Horvath, A. T., K. Misra, A. K. Epner, and G. M. Cooper. 2005–2015b. "Habit Formation, Craving, Withdrawal, and Relapse Triggers: Addictions' Effect on the Amygdala." http://www .communitycounselingservices.org/poc/view_doc.php?type =doc&id=48376&cn=1408.

Jay, J., and D. Jay. 2000. *Love First: A New Approach to Intervention for Alcoholism and Drug Addiction.* Center City, MN: Hazelden Information & Educational Services.

Jensen, F. 2015. *The Teenage Brain: A Neuroscientist's Survival Guide to Raising Adolescents and Young Adults.* New York: Harper.

Johnson, V. E. 1986. *Intervention: A Step-by-Step Guide for Families and Friends of Chemically Dependent Persons.* Minneapolis: Johnson Institute Books.

Lopez-Quintero, C., J. Pérez de los Cobos, D. S. Hasin, M. Okuda, S. Wang, B. F. Grant, and C. Blanco. 2011. "Probability and Predictors of Transition from First Use to Dependence on Nicotine, Alcohol, Cannabis, and Cocaine: Results of the National Epidemiologic Survey on Alcohol and Related Conditions (NESARC)." *Drug and Alcohol Dependence* 115: 120–30.

McCoy, Krisha. 2009. "When Adult Addiction Affects Children." *Everyday Health.* http://www.everydayhealth.com/ addiction/when-adult-addiction-affects-children.aspx#.

McLellan, A. T., D. C. Lewis, C. P. O'Brien, and H. D. Kleber. 2000. "Drug Dependence, a Chronic Medical Illness: Implications for Treatment, Insurance, and Outcomes Evaluation." *Journal of the American Medical Association* 284: 1689–95.

National Alliance on Mental Illness. n. d. "Dual Diagnosis." https://www.nami.org/Learn-More/Mental-Health-Condi tions/Related-Conditions/Dual-Diagnosis.

National Association for Children of Alcoholics. n. d. "Children of Addicted Parents: Important Facts." http://www.nacoa.net /pdfs/addicted.pdf.

National Center on Addiction and Substance Abuse (CASA) at Columbia University. 2010. *Behind Bars II: Substance Abuse and America's Prison Population.* New York: CASA Columbia. http://www.centeronaddiction.org/addiction-research/ reports/substance-abuse-prison-system-2010.

———. 2011. *Adolescent Substance Use: America's #1 Public Health Problem.* New York: CASA Columbia. http://www .centeronaddiction.org/addiction-research/reports/adolescent -substance-use.

National Council on Alcoholism and Drug Dependence. n. d. "Family History and Genetics." Accessed January 27, 2015. https://ncadd.org/aboutaddiction/family-history-and -genetics.

National Institute on Drug Abuse. 2002. *Research Report Series: Therapeutic Community.* NIH Publication Number 02–4877. http://archives.drugabuse.gov/pdf/RRTherapeutic.pdf.

———. 2005. *Research Report Series: Marijuana.* NIH Publication Number 15–3859, revised September 2015. https:// d14rmgtrwzf5a.cloudfront.net/sites/default/files/mjrrs_9_15 .pdf.

———. 2007. *Drugs, Brains, and Behavior: The Science of Addiction.* NIH Pub No. 14–5605, revised July 2014. https://d14rmg trwzf5a.cloudfront.net/sites/default/files/soa_2014.pdf.

———. 2008. *Principles of Drug Addiction Treatment,* 3rd ed. NIH Publication No. 12–4180, revised December 2012. https://d14rmgtrwzf5a.cloudfront.net/sites/default/files /podat_1.pdf.

———. 2012. "DrugFacts: Understanding Drug Abuse and Addiction." *DrugFacts.* http://www.drugabuse.gov/publica tions/drugfacts/understanding-drug-abuse-addiction.

———. 2014. "What to Do If Your Teen or Young Adult Has a Problem with Drugs." Accessed June 15, 2015. http://www. drugabuse.gov/related-topics/treatment-research/if -teen-or-young-adult-has-drug-abuse-problem.

Sandor, R. 2009. *Thinking Simply about Addiction: A Handbook for Recovery.* New York: Jeremy P. Tarcher/Penguin.

Simpson, D. D., G. W. Joe, and B. S. Brown. 1997. "Treatment Retention and Follow-up Outcomes in the Drug Abuse Treatment Outcome Study (DATOS)." *Psychology of Addictive Behaviors* 11: 294–307.

Straussner, S. L. A., and H. Byrne. 2009. "Alcoholics Anonymous: Key Research Findings from 2002–2007." *Alcoholism Treatment Quarterly* 27: 349–67.

Substance Abuse and Mental Health Services Administration. 2010. *Results from the 2009 National Survey on Drug Use and Health: Volume I. Summary of National Findings.* NSDUH Series H-38A, HHS Publication No. SMA 10–4586 Findings. Rockville, MD: Office of Applied Studies.

————. 2014. *Results from the 2013 National Survey on Drug Use and Health: Summary of National Findings*. NSDUH Series H-49, HHS Publication No. (SMA) 14–4863. Rockville, MD: Substance Abuse and Mental Health Services Administration.

Treffert, M. 2008. "Are You Someone's Puppet? Four Ways People Manipulate Others." *Boundaries 4 Codependents* (blog). Accessed March 15, 2015. http://codependentboundaries .blogspot.com/2008/08/are-you-someones-puppet-four-ways .html.

Trimpey, J. 1996. *Rational Recovery: The New Cure for Substance Addiction*. New York: Pocket Books/Simon and Schuster.

Trudeau, M. 2010. "With Drinking, Parent Rules Do Affect Teens' Choices." NPR Morning Edition, May 31. http://www .npr.org/templates/story/story.php?storyId=127222042.

Vanderplasschen, W., K. Colpaert, M. Autrique, R. C. Rapp, S. Pearce, E. Broekaert, and S. Vandevelde. 2013. "Therapeutic Communities for Addictions: A Review of Their Effectiveness from a Recovery-Oriented Perspective." *Scientific World Journal* 427817. DOI: 10.1155/2013/427817.

Winters, K. C., T. Fahnhorst, A. Botzet, S. Lee, and B. Lalone. 2012. "Brief Intervention for Drug-Abusing Adolescents in a School Setting: Outcomes and Mediating Factors." *Journal of Substance Abuse Treatment* 42: 279–88.

Acknowledgments

To Jed Wallace, Marisa Solís, and David Hayward for your guidance and expertise in making this dream a reality.

To Randi, who stood by my side with the skill of a hummingbird.

To my staff at PB, who believed in our journey.

To the countless families and clients who taught me that anything is possible.

To Chris, whose courageous battle took me on a lifelong journey of gratitude.

To my mom, my biggest cheerleader.

To my children, whom I love more than life itself.

Thank you. This is for you.

Robin Barnett, EdD, LCSW, is a respected behavioral health expert and former CEO of Park Bench Group Counseling, a progressive addiction rehabilitation facility in Northfield, NJ, which she cofounded in 2006. A licensed clinical alcohol and drug counselor, and a certified sex addiction expert and therapist, for nearly two decades she has helped countless people conquer addictive behavior and a multitude of behavioral challenges. Inspired by firsthand experience when her own brother encountered a downward spiral with alcoholism and drugs, Barnett hopes to help others manage the heartache of this struggle by sharing her professional—and personal—insights. Barnett is a well-known resource in the clinical community. She was named among "America's Best Therapists" by *Psychology Today*, and has appeared as a drug, alcohol, and behavior expert on various national media outlets, including MTV, CNN, HLN, NBC, FOX, ABC (*20/20, Nightline*), and CBS. Barnett is a regular on *The Steve Wilkos Show* (NBC Universal Syndication) as their substance abuse expert, and is currently included in the fabric of several unscripted television projects. Barnett holds a doctorate in human services administration from the University of Sarasota and a master's in social work from Rutgers, the State University of New Jersey. Barnett resides with her family at the Jersey Shore.

Foreword writer **Darren Kavinoky** is cocreator and host of the hit television show *Deadly Sins* on Investigation Discovery (ID). He is the cohost of *Did He Do It?* and the featured "criminal interventionist" on *Breaking Point*, also on the ID network. Kavinoky is also a certified interventionist, attorney and legal analyst, and "misbehavior" expert who appears regularly on *The Today Show, The View, Entertainment Tonight, The Insider, Dr. Phil, Dr. Drew*, CNN, HLN, Fox News, and many other TV and radio shows.

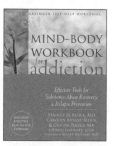

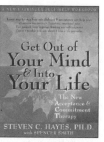